BREAKING
BARRIERS

YOUR GUIDE TO PERSONAL MASTERY

authorHOUSE®

AuthorHouse™
1663 Liberty Drive, Suite 200
Bloomington, 1IN 47403
www.authorhouse.com
Phone: 1-800-839-8640

First published by AuthorHouse   3/23/2009

ISBN: 978-1-4389-6488-1 (sc)

Printed in the United States of America
Bloomington, Indiana

This book is printed on acid-free paper.

DEDICATION

Dedicated to my parents, Marcy and Cliff Becker who
have always been there to guide me in my life through
love and positive growth.

ACKNOWLEDGEMENTS

As with any great undertaking you quickly begin describing success as "we" and not "me" or "I". This is truly the case in the year it has taken to complete the thoughts transcribed on the following pages. It is only the efforts of the many that make things like this happen. I would especially like to thank my wife Misti for her support and love throughout writing this book.

In addition I would like to thank Debbie, for reviewing and discussing key points of the project. Chaz, a close friend who brought clarity to the descriptions I created. Bingo, for the countless hours of direction and understanding, making the book stronger and balanced. To the students of the Southbury Academy of Karate, who, over the years, have given me an opportunity to analyze and develop so many areas of personal performance training. To my family and friends Trevor, Megan, Laura, Dan, Peter, John, Keith and Joe who listened to my ideas and have been helpful in so many ways.

I am grateful to all that I have been given,

Sincerely,

Leif Becker

BREAKING BARRIERS

YOUR GUIDE TO PERSONAL MASTERY

LEIF MANCHESTER BECKER

CONTENTS

PREFACE

Over the years I've appeared on a variety of TV shows, including *Late Show With David Letterman* and have lectured on the martial arts field to a variety of audiences. Generally, most audience members are interested in learning how practical aspects of martial arts might be adapted to everyday living.

Can martial arts help jump-start personal productivity or contribute to self-discovery? I believe there are many useful lessons that spring from martial arts and these are easily adapted for nearly any person's everyday life.

Invariably, right before I am introduced, there will be a mention of several key accomplishments, including my achieving World Record Status. Truthfully, I really don't place a great deal of value in titles. That's because it is not *what* I have achieved that I hope to share with you. Instead I am interested in sharing something else: the person I've become and the person I continue to strive to be.

The focus I bring to my everyday life has come through a deep level of training. But only through the rigors of training, did I have a "breakthrough" of sorts one day. I realized that it is not the *physicality* of what I am doing or even the strain I endure while I perform martial arts that is important. Rather the challenge rests with *who I am at that moment.*

Martial arts is my window through which I searched to give direction to my life.

Like most students in school, I hadn't a clue as to how I would earn a living. At the age of sixteen, when I stumbled on an early martial arts class, somehow I could begin to visualize myself differently and I was enthusiastic about the possibilities. And it was nearly a dozen or more years before I began to develop clarity about my progression in the field. It was as if the window through which I viewed life suddenly became clearer and I could see ahead to distant vistas.

Each of us may have our own portal to view life and identify our aspirations, goals and dreams.

If you haven't a clue as to where your passion may be found, this book is designed to help give you greater clarity. If you already feel you've found your niche but lack the momentum at times to drive yourself forward with a higher degree of satisfaction and purpose, I hope this book shows you the path towards greater fulfillment. In either case, self-discovery is a wonderful journey and one that is best traveled every day, for an entire lifetime!

I realize the window through which you view the world is likely very different from mine and very different from that of every other person. But I believe our outcome remains the same. We both stand on the precipice of the person we are in the present moment. And the person each of us is about to become. With each day comes the possibility of enlightenment and change.

Often we perceive barriers. Most of us feel these barriers stop us from becoming who we need to be.

Truth? Each of us is fully capable of breaking through those barriers, nearly all of which are self-imposed. This book is written to facilitate personal change, no matter how that change is defined. Growth may be through the world around us, such as seeking to become a more loving spouse, or a better parent, or even a more involved coworker or a stronger friend. On another level, the growth may be more introspective and internal. Perhaps your growth is best expressed through actions of patience, confidence, courage, vision, self-control, and/or balance.

Ready? Start today! You have an entire lifetime ahead of you. For some that "entire lifetime" may be measured in years, for others the timeline could equate to many decades. But for each of us, time is really not a practical yardstick. The true measurement is found in personal growth.

Finally, words can be powerful tools. It's true: "The pen is mightier than the sword." Over the years, I have found great wisdom and inspiration through a collection of quotes. Though I know many by heart, I still enjoy re-reading them. I have placed a collection of my favorite quotes at the end of this book. And what might you find at the end of "The End?" Bruce Lee. He has proven to be a wonderful personal inspiration. His words seem a fitting way to conclude this book, which, on some level, all began for me when I entered the world of martial arts as a teenager.

I am wishing you every success!

Leif Becker

1

"Ever since I was a child I have had this instinctive urge for expansion and growth. To me, the function and duty of a quality human being is the sincere and honest development of one's potential."

—Bruce Lee

YOUR THREE
ENERGIES

What is Self-Mastery? Self-Mastery is a special and individualized means that permits a person to take charge of his or her life. It's that simple.

In a state of Self-Mastery *you* steer your day-to-day existence, thwarting negative influences before they take hold. When something (even somebody) seeks to produce unwelcome elements of stress in your life, Self-Mastery permits you to return to a harmonious state of well-being. The stressful situation may prevail but through Self-Mastery one is able to re-direct thoughts and simply "step" into a balanced state. Through Self-Mastery, your life unfolds in the present moment as you make choices that deliver fulfillment.

Like many important lessons, there is an underlying simplicity to Self-Mastery. In this book, I hope you'll realize there is no need to over-complicate several of the ideas I

1

offer. And Self-Mastery is one of those easy-to-understand concepts.

Self-Mastery is not possible without understanding what I call "The Three Energies." Energy is simply the ability or capacity to make things happen and the three energies I am describing can be found in the *physical, mental* and *spiritual* realms of each individual.

The easiest energy for most people to immediately understand is physical energy. When I give a talk about Martial Arts people instantly understand physical energy. Yup, I'm the guy who broke all of those boards and did it within the shortest time ever recorded. My World Record, on one level, is in fact a testament to physical energy.

But the irony for most people to understand—and why I wrote this—is that physical energy is only *one* of *three* profoundly important energies available to each of us. And if I had not mastered the other two energies—mental and spiritual—I would not have succeeded in earning the World Record. Further, without appreciating the three energies, I would have no claim to understanding Self-Mastery and why it represents the life force behind leading a fulfilling life.

PHYSICAL ENERGY

Because we are a nation that enjoys watching sports, it's easier to identify physical energy. The Olympics are an obvious display of physical energy and we marvel how the human body can perform in such spectacular ways. Although most of us are not Olympians, we can nevertheless see signs of effective physical energy management by certain individuals who perform effortlessly **throughout the day.** They know when to conserve their energy and when to expend it. And they seem to do so without dependence upon caffeine, sugar, or cigarettes.

Although outside stimulants may appear to offer some people a "boost in free energy," in reality the body is forced out of balance. As a result, the body has to expend more energy to manage the imbalance caused by the quick fixes. In simplest terms, Self-Mastery recognizes that when the body feels fatigued, it's time to rest.

Since physical energy can be seen in the body's strength and endurance, what can you do now to bring your physical energy to optimal levels? Every person has different needs and is able to perform due to his or her own personal physical capabilities. What is your current physical program to keep your body's energy performing at its best? If you are interested in Self-Mastery, you will need to develop your own individualized plan to maximize your physical energy.

Instead of relying on a myriad of quick espresso breaks or a carb-sugar fix, the best way to master one's physical energy is to choose options such as frequent exercise and practicing self-renewing and revitalizing skills that prevent the accumulation of stress.

MENTAL ENERGY

Once in a while, I come across a science story that is hard to believe. That's how I felt when I read a reliable and highly researched story about stroke sufferers being able to operate computers, write e-mails, and drive wheelchairs *with nothing but their thoughts*. Their mental energy alone triggered the action. Dr. Jonathan Wolpaw, at New York State's Department of Health Wadsworth Center, has developed a program which allows people to write text on the computer purely by thinking of letters one at a time. The program permits severely paralyzed individuals to use their brain signals to send commands to a computer, allowing them to communicate independently.

This mental energy is completely independent of muscle control or what I call "physical" energy and such pivotal ground-breaking work by Dr. Wolpaw and his fellow researchers helps underscore the power of the human mind.

If you want a solid definition of mental energy, that's it!

Just as physical energy comes from diet, exercise and rest, our mental energy stems from our thoughts and now we know unequivocally that the mind can manifest energy unlike we ever imagined before. And while it is critically important to keep the mind agile via a variety of interesting mental exercises, giving the brain the nutrition it needs and seeking to stay in a "learning mode" in order to impart plasticity to prevent early aging, it is also equally important to be aware of the random thoughts that percolate through our minds, dictating emotional responses that may not serve our best interests.

Our mental energy can permit us—through personal choices—to live in a positive and healthy way. It makes us feel inspired, hopeful, self-confident, playful, loving and in touch with those areas that matter most.

One of the better approaches to maximizing mental energy is through the art of visualization. I call it an art because the process has to be practiced a bit, though many people can develop this "art" quickly. Visualization is creating a mental picture so that your brain can see the healthy possibilities more clearly.

A simply analogy to grasp the power of visualization is to think of today's television screen technology. High-definition viewing is here. In a few years we may enjoy something called Super Hi-Resolution, an ultra viewing experience that may offer remarkable detail differentiation. Now, if a person enters a large room with two viewing screens, one with high-resolution color while the other screen offers a scratchy, out-of-focus, black-and-white show, it is likely the person will walk to the screen with a clear, detailed, colorful show. If you were forced to watch the out-of-focus imagery, no doubt you'd begin to feel bored, antsy and unchallenged.

That's what visualization can do for you personally. With a clear, colorful projection of a meaningful and engaging image of your goal, you, too, will move in that direction.

In simplest terms, seeing yourself already working in the career you want actually helps your brain both *imagine and visualize* that attaining that goal is possible. Focusing consistently on a goal will enable you to manifest it far sooner than if you did not visualize. Without visualization, you can become impatient, bored, lose your direction and eventually feel empty.

Visualization works. Now commonly called "manifesting," growing research underscores that visualizations are increasingly effective in helping people to focus their unlimited mental energy. Harnessing your mental energy will help produce Self-Mastery.

Spiritual Energy

The existence of subtle, spiritual energy was well known to the ancient traditions of many early civilizations. Today, for some people "spiritual energy" takes on a religious meaning. But I wish to be clear: I am not speaking of religion when I address spiritual energy, though for some people, spiritual energy is strengthened and directed through his or her religious belief.

In some ways, spiritual energy involves the inner core of a person; some might call it the soul. When spiritual energy is tapped—at least this is true for *me*—one begins to grasp aspects of life in a new, more profound manner. There is a shift in the core of one's being and this shift brings a new, clearer and more powerful understanding that helps trigger a transcendent growth.

I hope this book will help further your spiritual growth. For each individual, that spiritual path is completely unique so my recommending a specific plan—a one-size-fits-all— seems irresponsible. However, I can suggest that meditation helped me get started. And I believe it can also work for you.

As I learned to develop spiritual energy, I had to go beyond the conditioned, "thinking" mind—the pure mental energy state described in the above paragraphs. Through meditation, I began to approach a deeper state of relaxation or awareness. Meditation often involves turning simply to one basic idea or thought as one seeks to quiet the mind.

Again, a one-size-fits-all approach is meaningless. It would be impossible for me to point you towards the meditative practice that might serve you best. Different meditative disciplines encompass a wide range of spiritual methods. And each distinct method may emphasize different goals. These can vary from seeking a higher state of consciousness, to greater focus, to engendering creativity or to developing self-awareness. And there are methods which facilitate a more relaxed and peaceful frame of mind.

However, I do urge you to begin to explore your own spiritual energy since understanding and directing this third energy, too, is pivotal to achieving Self-Mastery.

WHAT PREVENTS
SELF-MASTERY?

If our primary energies are not aligned properly, we fail at Self-Mastery. One of the biggest hurdles to Self-Mastery is the nearly imperceptible *emotional resistance* each of us creates within ourselves.

What is emotional resistance? Again, we need not over-complicate the theory. I say emotional resistance is simply the force that keeps your unhealthy habits firmly in place. You can't stand being alone, so you hang out with people you don't really even like or respect. Or you're feeling a bit down, so eating something (even though you're not hungry) seems to dispel your anxiety. Is the force really imperceptible? I say yes. For most people, emotional resistance is hidden and goes undetected.

Self-discovery is the best trip you may embark on at anytime. That exciting adventure begins by throwing light on personal resistance. Take time as you read this book to see where your emotional resistance begins to nudge you off track. Since it can manifest itself in countless ways, here's a quick roundup of those strategies that seem to weaken emotional resistance:

Follow through on what you promise to do. Forgive others. Forgive yourself and move on. Express gratitude on an hourly basis. Write letters to those who have hurt you terribly. Just don't mail the letters. Live without expectation and stay

*present. Don't judge. Listen more than you speak. Let go of
your ego. Stop whining.*

And the most effective strategy? Draw positive energy
into your life by choosing to live one entire day without
criticizing anything.

ALIGNMENT: THE SECRET TO SELF-MASTERY

If you've ever picked up a pair of binoculars belonging to
another person to watch a game or concert, it's likely you
had to fiddle with the pair until the object you wanted to
see came into focus. Alignment of the three energies is
about the same thing.

The premise of alignment is simple. Making alignment
work on your behalf is more challenging; some would say
it is pretty much a lifetime process. But once you become
aware of the three energies, you then must discover how
you can make each of the three energies serve you best.

For instance, if you spend more of your time seeking
to develop your physical energy, you may inadvertently
neglect your spiritual energy. You're working too hard on
a major client presentation. The late hours stretch over a
week. No surprise, did you neglect your physical energy?
In this instance, it is wise to make an adjustment—or

implement alignment—so that the flow of your three energies equalize.

I have written an entire Chapter on Balance. When it comes to Self-Mastery, alignment is equally important. In sum, the three energies are really no different than a set of personal gears. Be aware of your energy flow across the physical, mental and spiritual realms that define you as a unique individual. It is your personal responsibility to know when each of the three energies may need a periodic adjustment so that alignment increases your well-being.

"As long as I can remember I feel I have had this great creative and spiritual force within me that is greater than faith, greater than ambition, greater than confidence, greater than determination, greater than vision. It is all these combined. My brain becomes magnetized with this dominating force which I hold in my hand."

—Bruce Lee

Circle of Mastery:

I have included a diagram of the Circle of Mastery. It was created through my years spent Mastering Board Breaking. Listed are the three energies discussed in this chapter as well as 6 steps to reaching mastery. I created it to help individuals understand their personal level of performance and understand what to look for when rating personal performance on a scale of 1 -10.
If you rate your level of achievement at a 1, 2 or 3 you are working in the area of Memorization.

If you rate your level of achievement at a 4, 5 or 6 you are working in the area of Practice.

If you rate your level of achievement at a 7, 8 or 9 you are working in the area of Performance.

If you rate your level of achievement at a 10 you are working in the area of Mastery.

Lifes Circle to Mastery

Personal Mastery Equation

2

"*The fate of a people depends much more on their character than on their intelligence.*"

—Gustave Le Bon

CHARACTER

SMALL BUNDLE

We all have been told that positive self-esteem is the true linchpin to success. Without confidence, who can succeed?

So I'd like to introduce a newer strategy and one that I needed to learn while developing my strength in martial arts. Consider this: Confidence, especially when one believes he or she is absolutely correct, can make a person inflexible. Sometimes an overly confident person doesn't appear to be an equal among co-workers, friends and colleagues. That's because the overly confident person may, at times, stand *above* others. So I am going to suggest something different than constantly conveying a clear style of strong confidence.

Instead, understand the value of an unassuming nature. If you are down to earth (dare I say humble?), you can view life with an openness that likely will bring new learning each day. I believe a certain modesty, yes *humility*; will serve you well. Benjamin Franklin once said, "A man all wrapped up in himself makes a very small bundle."

In many ways, I believe modesty is a far superior demeanor. And the irony is that a humble approach to life may make you far more effective *than confidence alone*. Much of my philosophy is about creating balance. Humility is a necessary component for personal equilibrium and your success.

Here's why:

Being humble permits you to learn. When you're honest with your performance, you have a greater chance of assessing your mistakes, correcting them and moving on.

You can avoid the pitfall of blaming others and falling into the trap I call "being- right-you're-wrong".   Pointing fingers cultivates a false sense of pride. False pride is the polar opposite of self-esteem and often masks itself as confidence.

Being humble permits you to understand people better.

Humility gives you the power to concentrate more on self-control and self-discipline. As you learn balance, humility makes you flexible. Consider this from Tao Te Ching:

> *"When a man is living,*
> *He is soft and supple.*

When he is dead,
He becomes hard and rigid."

Humility keeps suppleness and flexibility alive in each of us. It permits us to wisely sharpen our perception and thus improve performance.

CLASS

Here in the United States we enjoy what people identify as a classless society—certainly in comparison to other places in the world. Naturally our definition of class can vary versus other societies, and it may also vary from region to region. But in traveling and speaking around the nation, one quickly sees that class has nothing to do with money. True, here in America we often confuse class with money since we place a good deal of value on personal wealth. There is a different wealth found in true class.

Let me give you *my* definition of class. Class is an aura of polite and understated sure-footedness, which allows a person to assess a situation without being overbearing and cocky.

Class is derived from self-discipline and self-knowledge. Class quietly shows up one day when you have proved to *yourself* that you can meet the heart-wrenching trials of life head on and *not run away scared.*

This well-earned self-knowledge has a decidedly transformative effect on how you treat others as well. A person with class is not a braggart. Class does not gloat and does not seek to win every argument. And when there's a discussion, debate or even a heated argument, class has no need to diminish another's point of view or ridicule the other person. People with class don't roll their eyes when someone is making a heartfelt suggestion, especially when the idea appears to be "off the wall" or unconventional.

In my years of martial arts training, the true masters could demonstrate a high level of class through victory. And, equally important, through defeat! It's important for all of us to accept victory professionally and humbly. And the same is true for defeat.

How do you accept defeat? Sure, you can detest defeat and hate losing, but having a classy approach to any setback or any defeat precludes you from becoming a poor sport.

Ego Versus Spirit

Can you operate from a mindset that embraces both ego and spirit simultaneously? I don't think so. Ego is a mechanism that continually works to shore up our sense of self- worth, especially versus others. Ego operates on bravado and fear. Ego makes us judgmental, selfish, unforgiving, pretentious and competitive in a wrong-headed way. Ego not only feeds a strong desire to win at all costs, ego delights in the other person *losing*. Ego makes us quickly prone to frustration.

Spirit is the opposite. Spirit encourages us to be tolerant, calm, entertain win/win propositions. Spirit is selfless, creative, loving, and nonjudgmental. Spirit is fed by love, abundance, generosity, and kindness. But in the presence of fear? Spirit dies.

The next time you're in a situation that tests your patience, carefully observe how your ego enters the situation and attempts to hijack your actions. One of the hardest lessons in life for many to learn is permitting only the spirit to take over when a situation begins to deteriorate.

Spirit cannot exist when you are feeling frustrated. When things get off track, and when running late and trying 'catch up' when you're running late, slow down. Explore why you're in this situation. I guarantee you have been placed there simply because there is something you need to learn about spirit. Until you permit spirit to take over, you will be doomed to repeat this scenario in all of its varied and exhausting forms over and over again. Conversely, when your spiritual energy is permitted to thrive, you live with the joy of Self-Mastery.

THE PATH TO STRENGTHEN PERFORMANCE

It's hard to pursue what you love—and cheerfully succeed— when your heart is filled with anger, retribution and revenge. Don't carry around an agenda of getting even. Remember, needing to be right is the ego working against your spirit. Recently I noticed that an ordinary, everyday phrase is on the upswing. Without much thought, many of us pepper everyday observations with, "Oh I hate that!" referring to some little trivial incidence that may occur on a daily basis. "I hate the rush hour," or "I hate Bob interrupting all the time." Hate? Isn't that a bit of an overreaction?

I have witnessed some truly great athletes perform at peak. Athletes come in all sorts of shapes, sizes, mental attitudes and competitive forms and the ones I am thinking about are rare and exceptional because of their love and passion. I believe these exceptional athletes understand that mental toughness and strength come from a certain positive enthusiasm each has for the task at hand and for the greater good of the sport. They love what they do. They perform with true passion; there is no room for hate.

They approach the sport with healthy fervor and ardor. They're about passion and not bent on getting even. They also have an equal passion for the people with whom they interact; yes, even their toughest competitors. Their heightened awareness somehow helps them compete more freely, without the baggage of revenge and seeking to set right past wrongs.

Understand the power of forgiveness. When you forgive, you actually let go of the very things; those self-limiting negative emotions that hold you back. Having negative feelings and seeking to one-up the next person will only trample success when it comes to your door. But with a heart filled with passion, unfettered by anger, your performance will be markedly strengthened.

If you look within yourself and still feel pain caused by others *in the past*, be it yesterday or ten years ago, explore the irony of your choice. Why choose to carry the negative baggage of past pain? How will that serve you?

Instead, forgive. Let it go. Forgiveness is the true path to strengthen your performance.

GENEROSITY OF SPIRIT

If you think of yourself as a giving person, have you ever thought about why you give? Some profess the pleasure is simply enjoying the reaction of others, seeing the grin on their faces. Do you give to receive something in return? Many of us do.

You can learn a lot from people who tend to give freely because their offerings are made without reservation. Surround yourself with generous people—and not for the reason that one young student suggested to me, "You'll get more!" Instead, observe truly generous people, and you'll find their *spirit* is catching.

People with true generosity have a different outlook on life: They give because they feel it is the right thing to do. And they have the sense that resources at their fingertips will never dry up. They look around and see abundance, even when things might be pretty grim and desperate.

When it comes to giving, don't think only in terms of money. Here are things many of us may give another person. And it won't cost you a cent:

A kind word for a job well done. Genuine praise is a precious commodity.

A free exchange of information; don't hoard knowledge, statistics or data that may only benefit you.

Offer someone comfort in time of need.

Why not pitch in when a colleague seems overwhelmed by a deadline?

Roots

Every world record holder or star athlete starts out as an amateur. All of us begin this way. But those exceptional few who later emerge with a prized trophy or desired achievement have a happy way of valuing where they came from. They honor their roots. They fondly recall, too, those who helped them along the way.

Recalling where you started can also keep you grounded. It helps engender empathy for others who may be struggling and reminds us that we never quite outgrow the need to master a new skill.

So as you move ahead, don't forget your beginnings and try to stay connected to those who helped boost your rise. Be grateful and give back to the community in which you got your start.

When I've aired this notion in lectures—honoring your roots—some people have told me their early days were filled with trauma, and they'd rather *not* give those tough times a second thought.

Clearly I'm not suggesting it's a useful exercise to focus on tough times and re-live pain. In fact, that's exactly what not to do. Dwelling on past pain is a non-constructive process that will only serve to stir up more struggles and make you a magnet for attracting more negative energy.

Instead, I am suggesting something completely different: Honoring your roots can reinforce a belief in your personal worth and help lay the foundation for increased psychological momentum to propel you over the next hurdle. If your early days were defined by poverty or any other rough challenge, even a difficulty in learning, that's a good thing. Tough times shape all of us. Rather than burying the memory of where you came from, let it help generate strength. Let it sensitize you to the struggles and challenges others may face.

Whether your past is looked at as good or bad (or perhaps happy or sad), it is your own personal history. It is there to teach you something. If you have to re-examine your past, do so only for the lesson it teaches *you*.

Individuals who continually relive memories over and over again are making a choice to dwell in the past without learning the lesson. Because they live in the world of yesterday, they are unable to realize goals today. Let go of the emotions attached to past. In this way, you will allow yourself to stay present, grow and move closer to important goals.

A Few Simple Truths

A number of philosophical ideas that govern Western Civilization—many truths that we live by today—were explored by scholars in ancient Greece and Rome. It must have been wonderful speaking about these lofty ideas, gazing out at the blue Aegean, trying to figure out the meaning of life.

Today we get to live them! No matter where you are in life, there are several values; character-defining truths that you cannot compromise on or give short shrift to. When we see a great political leader fail or witness the life of a beloved reel out of control, invariably the person somehow compromised one of these important values.

A life worth living invariably asks us to re-examine each of these when we need to make a critical choice. Here are three that I feel can never be compromised:

Honesty is the first building block of character. If at a time you find yourself challenged and at risk of losing everything, never lose your desire to be honest in all of your dealings. The more scrupulous you are, the more difficult it is to look the other way and to manipulate a deal or an important agreement to your clear—and unfair—advantage. Any success you seek must be earned honestly and without a shred of injustice or duplicity. It is better to lose all and preserve your character. A sports title, a promotion, year-end bonus, or even a bid on a piece of real estate is not worth a cent if you've sought it through dishonest means.

Make your success depend on character and drive your decisions with honesty. And even if you are at risk of losing out on a big promotion or choosing an action that may be unpopular with your family or friends, remember that remaining honest and true to your character is a choice. Character is the real fortune.

And the one thing you cannot let fail is *your conscience*. For instance, your view of a situation may not be accurate, thus your view or perspective may fail you. Even logical choices may not work in your favor at times. There will be times when your normally rationale demeanor somehow fails you. But a solid conscience never fails. Pride yourself on being open and straightforward.

Here's the correlation. Maintaining a high level of concentration and intensity relies on a pure sense of clarity and an internal focus. If you rely on your conscience, then you, too, *do not care about what others think*. Amateurs starting out in martial arts often attach value to how others perceive them. They fret too much about their stance and form. They wonder, "Do I look serious enough? Did that move appear awkward, even foolish?"

And so it is with life and learning to rely on your conscience. If you make a decision that is incongruent with your values, if you fail to do the right thing, you'll suffer. You can fool others but at the end of the day, you can never fool yourself.

Work Ethic. People who succeed at life, ***everyday*** champions if you will, enjoy hard work. Period. They don't look for short cuts. In fact top athletes thrive when things begin to look tough. That's when the enthusiasm starts! They become eager and feed on the challenge. If you wish to succeed and boost your output, examine how you approach your job and getting the work done.

For comparison purposes, think of the millions of immigrants who came to America from foreign countries. They may not have spoken the language here, but the majority were willing to roll up their sleeves and get the job done. They were grateful to have work. Many came from places where there was no opportunity, no chance to succeed, no food on the table. They were hungry. A solid work ethic helped make this country—and many other places in the world—great and wildly successful. You're going to need that very same solid work ethic. Stay hungry.

Everyday champions don't skimp or do just enough to get by. Conversely, they certainly don't adopt the mindless workaholic ethic. Never take pride in staying late to shuffle papers around, on the off chance someone important may notice. Do what it takes to do the best job, don't cut corners, and approach your work with enthusiasm and gratitude.

All successful people I've coached never *begrudge* the hard stuff. They don't complain or resist going the extra mile. They don't resent staying late. That's because they know that carrying even the smallest amount of resentment will instantly set up an invisible wall of resistance. It halts opportunity from heading your way. If you're willing to go that extra mile, a steady stream of prospects and exciting new opportunities will flow your way.

Own it. If most people learned of a stupendous inheritance, say a truly desirable and perfect gift—perhaps millions of dollars or a beautiful, expense-free tropical retreat in the Pacific, most people would cheerfully accept the inheritance, right? Who wouldn't want to "own" those circumstances?

There are many things we own in life. Yet most of us think of ownership in terms of property. There's a more challenging ownership I'd like you to re-think.

If you can master this new proprietary interest, I can personally guarantee there will be no stopping you.

Ready?

When the roof springs a leak, when someone else gets the promotion, when things happen that we lump together as "unfair," don't resist the change. Instead, accept it and **own it.** Yes, take a proprietary interest. Deal with the situation and learn from it. Don't fight it! Bumped from an airline flight, with no options to get to your client meeting? Adapt and make good use of the new situation. Each day we may find ourselves addressing unexpected situations. In the next few weeks, become keenly aware of your reactions to unforeseen circumstances, especially when you're unhappy with the turn of events. Explore how you deal with the unexpected. Seek the best ways to address change in a positive manner. Stop complaining. Don't take pleasure in re-telling your woe-is-me-awful-put-upon circumstances over and over again to colleagues, friends and family. We complain to others about things we view to be unfair. Or we point a finger and place blame. Don't! All of that feeds the ego.

On the other hand, you need not sit silently with a smile on your face when unsatisfactory circumstances suddenly appear and challenge you. If you're looking forward to a delicious meal and the restaurant offers lousy service or bad food at upscale prices, you don't have to sit there and cheerfully accept it. The true challenge will be how you handle the lousy service or bad food. Don't escalate to anger, don't accuse and start wagging your finger.

Why not simply point out the situation in a neutral way and seek to make the situation better? *Be like water:* Let it flow through you.

If you can stay free of blaming others and letting anger seep into the situation, *balance will re-appear quickly.*

With balance comes joy. As Lao Tzu brilliantly phrased it:

"Serenity is the master of restlessness."

Playing it Safe

There are times when choices we make are unpopular with others. But when a decision is a critically important one, you cannot play it safe.

When the course is uncharted, you must be fearless. Billie Jean King spoke about the correlation between winning and the ability to put it all on the line and take a shot. She says, in describing an appropriate response to standing firm, "You have to be willing to get fired every day...." I like that! Imagine taking an unpopular stance about a new marketing campaign simply because you believe it is the right thing and running the risk of getting fired? Few people will run that risk. But you must. When a do-or-die situation presents itself, don't play it safe.

I began this chapter with a short observation on confidence. I believe if you can adapt the tools outlined throughout this entire chapter, these skills will deliver the type of confidence you will need to exceed your expectations. You will have to make tough choices as you grow. But you'll look back and see how worthwhile those choices were.

As Herman Cain has said;

"Success is not the key to happiness. Happiness is the key to Success. If you love what you are doing, you will be successful."

3

"All appears to change when we change."

—Henri Amiel

CHANGE

THE DYNAMICS
OF PERSONAL
TRANSFORMATION

What stops people from changing? If you talk to your friends and those colleagues you know fairly well, it's likely you know something about their desires and dreams. So many people *know what they want*; they're even willing to let us see into their dream world. They can visualize new-found success and even write out a plan to make it a reality. We often speak of the, "Some day, I'll…." You fill in the blank. Dreams are as varied as the people who imagine better ways to live their lives.

Why then are not more people satisfied? Certainly we all know lots of people who go through the motions of initiating change, but quickly the majority of them fall back into their usual routine. Some coaching experts call this daily routine, a person's "comfort zone."

But when I examined the statistics, I wondered why a researcher hasn't come up with a better phrase—comfort zone seems *way* off the mark.

The Gallup organization estimates that 71% of workers are not engaged—interested or fulfilled—in their career. Over 75% of new businesses struggle to succeed. Over 50% of couples are in risk of divorce. 70% of us live paycheck to paycheck. 47% of us are experiencing significant levels of stress in our lives, and most of us are far from the levels of health and fitness we desire.

Exhausting, isn't it? Why do so many choose to live this way?

Do you?

When I was working on setting a new record for speed, I had to call upon a special type of stamina and a variety of other physical strengths simply to begin a new training program. I knew I would be up against resistance in all of its forms. Resistance?

For some reason, that word—so key to understanding the multiple skill levels of martial arts—on a completely *new* meaning than it ever had before.

And that's when I stumbled upon something I'll call *Emotional Resistance*. Getting the body in shape is one challenge. Getting the mind to accept that challenge and undergo change? That was equally daunting.

THE ENEMY

I believe that I knew what Emotional Resistance was long before I came up with the phrase. That's because I could certainly see it in any number of clients I was coaching. It's not that I didn't have Emotional Resistance at the time in my life. We all do. And of course I had it. It's just that one can always see things more readily and clearly in others than we can see in ourselves.

But I wish to be clear about Emotional Resistance. It really is a very damaging human trait. It is toxic, habit forming, makes us self-destructive, and prone to self-sabotage. It's why people drink to excess, stuff themselves when they are no longer hungry, lash out at perfect strangers—and loved ones—and screw up royally when faced with sure-fire success. It's also why most people lead quiet lives of desperation. They don't have to flame out and self-sabotage to the point of making headlines; they just never get to achieve the dreams they had hoped for.

Emotional resistance is why people who must change, do not change.

YOU

I believe you, too, have the chance to embark on a new life, setting your own new speed record if you will. Now is the time to begin a life that is filled with meaningful change.

I have to be brutally honest: You will not undergo a meaningful personal transformation unless you fully grasp what Emotional Resistance is. You have to see it in all of its various and attractive disguises.

You must square off against Emotional Resistance, as if it were your worst enemy. Because it is.

But the irony of Emotional Resistance is that it *never truly appears to be toxic or destructive.* That's the trick of Emotional Resistance: It often appears to be a pal, a buddy, a panacea to life's troubles—and it always uses one pat phrase when you want to change: "Tomorrow."

That's right. It never tells you that you're going to die with the music still in you. It tells you that you will reach your dreams. Yes: You'll earn the Championship title. You'll become CEO. You'll earn the great fortune of a lifetime. You'll land the job you have always dreamed of, write the great screenplay. *Tomorrow.*

If you have ever tried to diet, change a bad habit, get into better shape, make a choice that requires great courage or organize a project that you've procrastinated about (for months or years!), you have experienced Emotional Resistance.

Here are some truths I have learned about Emotional Resistance:

It's good at rationalizing.
It easily distracts you.
It sells quick fixes.
It takes the easy way out.
It numbs the pain.
It never faces failure.
It believes in lousy luck.
It makes excuses.
It encourages emotional upheavals and feeds on drama.
It prefers excessive consumption: Shopping, food, alcohol, drugs.
It thrives on time-wasting opiates: gossip, mindless sex, chat rooms, *hours* of TV.
It prefers messiness so you can't find things.
It convinces you to stay with the tribe.
Time is of no consequence. There's always tomorrow.

If you hope to change, it is up to you to become keenly aware of Emotional Resistance—in all of its innocent disguises—and seek to rout it out so that you make space for changes.

> "They say that time changes things, but you actually have to change them yourself."
>
> —Andy Warhol

Change is not easy. But the rewards exceed any imagined joy you think you may experience. Here are 15 key strategies that have worked for me when I sought to make change. Try a few—or all. Find what works for you.

1 - REMEMBER THAT IT'S A PROCESS

Expect to work your way up, rather than expecting to develop and maintain perfection instantly. Pace yourself. Be human about any let-downs. Don't dwell on them; simply accept the occasional set back and move on. I repeat: It's a process, not an overnight event.

2 - PUNT

A little structure makes a big difference in changing behaviors: Plan. Keep track of what works. And what does not work. Change the plan if it isn't working. Revamp your approach and see if something else will work.

3 - Get Clear On What Is Important To You

Many changes fail because we begin to compromise values, those things we hold important. Before you invest in making a big change, take some time to get clear on what is really important to you. For example, you might think you want a promotion, but if that big job means more late hours—and that's a sacrifice you and your family are not willing to make at this time, then that promotion may not be in alignment with what you really value. When you know what is truly important to you, it is easy to create a vision for yourself that will result in far more fulfillment.

4 - Work Your Way Up

In setting goals for any new change, break the goal into half steps. If it's a new-get-in-shape-program, write down your ideal workout schedule—maybe your ideal is three times a week. But if you haven't worked out in a long time, divide your ideal in half. Make the three times a week into a "half step"—commit to every Wednesday instead.

5 - Leverage Your Unique Attributes. Know Your Strengths

When you go about making changes, build on what makes you unique. While it sounds simplistic, I have seen some very smart people pay too much attention to their short-comings. Don't! It's all about balance. Sure, you don't ignore personal weaknesses but *focus on your strengths and trade on them*. Strengths and talents empower us. For example, if you are starting a business and are very strong in the creative arena, but weak on administration, partner with people that are great at implementing and *leverage your creative skills. Make that your focus.*

6 - 21 Days

Most new behaviors become habits when we give ourselves a full 21 days to adopt and to adapt to the new program. Yes, it takes time. Again, don't aim for overnight success and end up with fast failure. Give yourself 21 days to "get into the program." And if takes you 35 days to achieve 21 successive days, great! Just get to the 21 successive day level and you're ready to continue building again.

To understand the background on why 21 days helps a new behavior become "a habit," we need only read more about Dr Maxwell Maltz who wrote the bestseller *Psycho-Cybernetics*. Originally a plastic surgeon, Maltz noticed that it took 21 days for amputees to cease feeling phantom sensations in the amputated limb. From further observations he found it took 21 days to create a new habit, thus the "21 Day Habit Theory" has become an accepted part of self-help programs.

Brain circuits take engrams (memory traces), and produce neuroconnections and neuropathways only if they are bombarded for 21 days in a row. Truthfully, many of my motivated clients seem to take fewer days. Others require more. But I urge you to find what timeline works for you. And stick with it!

7 - SPACE

Change is a bit like the stock market: It requires an investment. Instead of money, however, give yourself the space that change needs to mature and grow. If you are already feeling over-burdened by responsibilities and recognize you need to change, what can you eliminate? If you are running at 100% capacity, you'll have neither time nor energy to effect change. Free up some healthy space in your life.

8 - YOUR LIFE

Yes, it is *your* life. And welcome to it. Working at change is forever. And you know what? Forever is a good thing. Being in a rut, and keeping yourself there, is a slow, painful, and humiliating death. In the case of certain problem behaviors, say eating and exercising, maintaining healthy behaviors over a lifetime can actually be easier than finding continual ways to eliminate "bad" behavior. How many people repeatedly shame themselves—over decades, even complete lifetimes—and make light of the unhealthy things they deliberately do to themselves?

9 - 28 DAYS

Once you have adapted and have three weeks of success, continue with the current program and introduce another small change around 28 days. But recognize you arrived *via pacing and increments*. Continue to experiment with small, attainable goals, and add more steps—just keep them as *half steps*. As you complete each one, you gradually move toward the life you want. In fact, you hardly feel the discomfort of change that causes most people to fail. If you accept the fact that most people resist change, that you can accept your natural inclination to "fight" is part of the process, not a personal failing.

10 - REFRAME

One attempt at a change usually isn't enough. Most people try and fail several times before they successfully change. But often the ones who do change, know how to re-frame failed attempts: They call them practice sessions. Remember, the greatest sports records are set by men and women who failed more times than they succeeded. Yes, Babe Ruth struck out more times than he hit home runs.

11 - ANTICIPATE

There are a lot of potholes in the road to change. Anticipating trouble spots is like getting into your car and reaching for the seat belt. Know you'll hit rocky patches and think about ways to get around those spots. Rocky patches are not forever. Successful changes can be.

12 - ON EDGE

For most people, there is no comfortable way to effect a change. You'll be on edge at first. But there's good news: The discomfort is temporary.

13 - Yes, You're Different

What works for one person may not work for another. Great strides by friends or colleagues can be inspirational to use. Use them as role models. In fact, role models can galvanize true change in some people. But if a role model's approach doesn't work for you, find another approach and keep your eye on the inspired transformation.

14 - Reward Your Progress

You know what to do. Acknowledge your success. It's called an incentive, not self-sabotage.

15 - Paradox

The only constant in change is change itself—what worked yesterday may not work today or tomorrow. And that is the paradox, the implicit irony of change. Strategies for managing some of life's most taxing situations, say chronic disease, are nearly identical to everyday, easy strategies. If it's not working, change *the strategy*. And if your normally successful approach suddenly fails, it may not be you. Perhaps the strategy needs to be tweaked over time in response to new circumstances.

A Few Other Thoughts

Remember: Change isn't easy. But it's also completely feasible. Old weaknesses and insecurities that you managed to efficiently camouflage suddenly make themselves obvious again. The stress of change can even lower your immune system. I am very lucky to enjoy good health. I can't say I'm absolutely invincible, but I'm pretty strong and blessed with robust health. But I have learned that when the psyche gets taxed, often the body will respond. It will shut down as a means for the psyche to heal itself and prepare for battle.

If you recognize this, then you can accept what is only a momentary reflex. That's all it is. Be prepared for it. I have seen countless clients come down with the flu, experience piercing headaches or even mindlessly induce an injury as a coping mechanism to postpone facing the necessary change, especially when the change is imminent. Do your best to take care of yourself and keep going. It is a rite of passage: But I know you will come out on the other side.

> *"It is not the strongest of species that survives, nor the most intelligent, but the one most responsive to change."*
>
> —*Charles Darwin*

4

"No passion so effectually robs the mind of all its powers of acting and reasoning as fear."

—Edmund Burke

FEAR

FEAR AND FAILURE

This may seem out of left field, but here goes: I'm *not* a big proponent of TV. I discourage it for those clients interested in making positive changes. Why?

TV has a numbing effect and tends to make most people passive. Thus, if you want to aim for higher goals, you have to stay active and cultivate an active frame of mind.

But I make one exception: If you're interested in conquering fear, watch a short program on the animal kingdom.

Witness how wild animals live day to day. Observe their emotional range. Most animals, especially mammals, experience emotions as we do. There is joy in finding a muddy watering hole during a drought or a mother chimp's palpable suffering when her infant succumbs to a fatal disease.

In the midst of life threatening forces, animals *live in the present moment.* They move on. Animals don't fret about tomorrow, even in the face of spectacular threats. To be sure, they'll step out of harm's way: Fear will galvanize a herd of antelope when a pride of lions approaches. Or fear will cause an animal to freeze when a predator nears. Paralysis, like camouflage, serves as protection.

But when danger passes, animals get on with living. Be they prey or hunter, animals do not settle in for a night's rest by wringing their paws and worrying if they'll eat the next day.

Can we face fear and move on? Absolutely. And to reach your dreams, you must master fear *and embrace failure.*

My experience with a variety of peak performers has shown that most of them are courageous and intrepid. They do not let fear—or failure—impede their thinking. It doesn't mean they don't experience fear. And most of them fail more than they succeed, though the outside generally sees only their successes.

Peak performers achieve success by processing fear quickly, embracing failure. And moving on.

What is fear anyway? It's a personal **emotional** response to a specific threat and danger.

There's no need to complicate the concept and add multi-layers of psychology to get at the root of fear. Sure, most psychologists tend to distinguish fear from anxiety since anxiety typically occurs without any visible, real external threat. But I am combining fear and anxiety together since often they are tough to separate in real life and the distinction typically is irrelevant if you wish to make a change in your life.

Call it what you will, fearful emotions that hold us back from living our true purpose create a long laundry list of personal limitations: dread, worry, apprehension, terror, horror, alarm, panic, anguish, agitation, jitteriness, worry, nervousness, uneasiness, wariness, defensiveness.

That's quite a rich vocabulary arising out of thousands of years of human evolution, isn't it?

So, how may we rule these self-limiting emotions, so they do not rule us? Here are the steps that I recommend. A few require specific actions. And remember: If you don't take action, change will not occur.

First, I'd like you to write this quote out and carry it with you for the next week:

"We are what we think. All that we are arises with our thought.
With our thoughts, we make our world."

—*Buddha*

CHANGE YOUR THINKING. CHANGE YOUR LIFE.

How you think and what you believe give shape to your life. Sounds simple, doesn't it?

Why then is life such a challenge for some people? Their thoughts have made it so.

If you don't believe thoughts shape your life, it is likely that you attribute outside forces to having a greater influence. That's a pointless way of living your life. Why? For the most part, you cannot control outside forces. You can only respond to them.

Believe me on this one: Change your thinking and your outlook will change. Opportunities begin to show up. You can transform your life.

FEAR OF FAILURE OR FEAR OF SUCCESS

You've heard these two popular phrases and you may wonder, "Okay, which do I have? Which fear is limiting me?" Guess what? I don't think it matters a whole lot. Fear is fear. Both tend to manifest self-limiting choices that place you in a funk. You experience under-achievement, guilt, self-sabotage, even pessimism. I don't believe it makes much of a difference if you fear making a fool of yourself during a crucial marketing presentation (fear of failure) or if you fear having too much money—and all the misery that comes with wealth (fear of success).

What's important is that you wish to change. Hold onto to your desire to effect change. Here's how.

KNOW WHAT YOU'RE DEALING WITH

What triggers fear in you? You can't resolve an issue if you don't know what the specific challenge is. Fear manifests in different ways and I'd like you to simply become more aware of those triggers. Start writing the fear triggers down. Be aware of timing, too. Exactly when do you begin to feel a general unease and discomfort? When do you get sweaty palms? When do you find yourself postponing something, simply because 'dealing with it' makes you uneasy? When does your mind race, predicting terrible outcomes to an unknown challenge? The boss asks for volunteers to manage a new sales meeting and you cringe. What will others think of your suggestions? These emotional stalls happen when we need to tackle a challenge and yet fear the consequences. Begin to recognize these internal reactions. *Awareness is pivotal to change.*

Here's another useful yardstick: Procrastination. *What you postpone, is what you are refusing to deal with.* Identify the important ones. What things have you not tackled (and will cause profound regret) if you don't get to them? Don't die with your song still inside you.

So what are you procrastinating about? Say you wish to get into shape so you can feel better about yourself—and thus begin the interview process so you can finally leave your dead end job. If you keep putting it off until tomorrow, fear is driving you. Not laziness. And for all of those people who are waiting to "feel better" before they tackle their self imposed limits, here's a loud wake up call. The day of feeling better *never arrives*. Feeling better is directly tied to taking action. Don't wait. Waiting makes a person feel worse over time. Waiting, like postponement, triggers depression. Only action can break the cycle. Get to it.

DETERMINATION

Remember that opening remark about TV's passive effect? I suggested that you can't deal with fear by being passive. *Commit yourself to staying active while you resolve self-imposed limits.* You alone placed those self-imposed limits in your path. You'll remove them. Stay determined to move ahead.

Immediately following is my plan to keep determination alive, along with five critical steps. The great thing is that you can begin today to propel yourself forward.

GET MOVING!

How can a person embrace determination? Get moving! Part of the challenge is that some people are so deep into an emotional hole, they can't quite pull themselves out. Here's what I tell them: Fake it if you must, it's not really important. But start moving and begin *acting* more confident and courageous.

Begin *acting* more confident and more courageous, you'll actually trigger forward momentum. The following five steps will make you immediately feel better and help to dispel fears.

First, work on your posture. It may sound corny but begin by standing up straight—throughout the day, you'll begin to feel a surge of personal power. Pay attention to how you carry yourself. Walk with pride, no slumping, and no shuffling. Be aware of posture when you get tired. Muscle through the fatigue by improving your breathing and correcting your posture. Do it for 21 days.

Second, become more enthusiastic. The word enthusiasm is derived from the Greek word, enthousiasmos, which means to be inspired or possessed by a divine being. Enthusiasm is an incredibly powerful tool, like healthy dynamite—if there were such a thing. Enthusiasm creates forward motions, it combats fear and pessimism. Turn off the news and remove yourself from people who complain and whine or those who are sarcastic and cynical. They'll suck enthusiasm and positive energy right out of you within seconds. Enthusiasm is like any other skill: if it is continually practiced and exercised, it gets better. Left unattended, it degrades.

Third, be aware of energy flow around you. Again, it may sound corny but protect your space by surrounding yourself with peace and cheer for better harmony. Some people block the flow of the available energy around them with negative thought patterns as they expose themselves to worry, doubt, anger, fear, hatred, depression, etc. *Become acutely aware of your own energy field.* When you are frequently objecting, saying "no", or believe "I can't," you block the positive energy flow in your own space. Be aware of those boundaries, restrictions and limitations that have held you back. Stay open.

Fourth, get your act together! Messy work area? Clean up your desk. If there's clutter in your life, get rid of it. Clutter saps emotional energy and makes you a slave to things. You cannot permit new thinking, exciting new opportunities, positive energy to flow into your life if you have negative roadblocks of clutter. In martial arts, we have great respect for energy or what often is referred to as *chi*. Bruce Lee, one of my personal heroes, believed calmness and tranquility arrived when one is free from external objects. He said, "It's not the daily increase but daily decrease. Hack away at the unessential." You're about to change your life for the better, so start hacking away at the unessential.

Fifth, act the pro. Be the champion of your new determination. A true professional can lead people, even entire organizations, during times of great duress. A perfectly calm day quickly changes to utter chaos, as terrible threats and mounting pressure intrude. Do you cave and give into fear? That's when to act the pro. Jump in, show initiative and begin to lead. This "acting as if" has a magical effect; you can completely transform yourself in a few hours. This "acting as if" creates an internal sense of forward motion. Forward motion, in turn, continues to engender determination. Out of determination comes self-reliance. Out of self-reliance comes confidence.

As you adopt the above steps, the amazing thing, too, is that you'll begin to notice that people will respond to you in a more positive manner.

RE-DEFINE SUCCESS

Most people interpret success too narrowly. Let's say you need to move to another part of the country; you have to get out of your current market, simply because it offers no future growth. Keep your options open. Don't narrow your choices. Look at the overall new region as an open field. And play that open field. Apply to as many employers throughout the entire region as is humanly possible. What most people do is to narrow success early on. They set their sites on only one city, feeling, "That's the place I could be the happiest." Then they fixate on only one potential new employer, suggesting, "There's a company that promotes a lot, I'm a perfect match for them!" Already, by narrowing their choices, they have narrowed their chance for success. So when that one employer has no openings, they feel they have failed. Keep your definition of success wide open, stay fluid as you seek to make change.

WORD CHOICE

Be aware of the power of the words you chose to use when describing attempts that did not work out. What we tell ourselves has huge implications. There's no need to be negative. Here's a simple way to re-frame a failed attempt. Say, "I didn't get the result I wanted." Do not belittle the outcome or berate yourself. In fact, you need not even use the word failure. *You simply did not get the results you wanted.* Period.

EMBRACE FAILURE

Try something. It may work. It may not. If it doesn't work, find another strategy. Keep it easy and embrace failure. Make failure your teacher; it's how we learn to adapt. In fact, without mini glitches, the life force we identify as 'evolution' could not have occurred. All living forms learned to adapt.

If you aren't willing to make mistakes or "fail," then you aren't willing to learn. If you don't learn, you don't grow. And, if you don't grow, what happens? You stagnate.

Watch a toddler as he or she learns to walk. No one says, "Oh well, he fell down, I guess he won't make a good walker." Be a toddler in life if you must. Learning through failure, too, keeps you young. If you wish to change, then be willing to be a novice all over again. It may appear to be a radical thought but I hope you learn how to enjoy making mistakes. All top performers do.

FAIL WITH GRACE

In martial arts, it is extremely important to learn how to take a fall and to recover gracefully. It's true, too, in many sports that rely on speed. Have you ever watched an Olympic ice skating champ take a spectacular fall? Even in the face of pain, gold medalists get right back up and demonstrate grace under pressure. No one enjoys watching a sore loser. Often they blame other elements. Be graceful in defeat. It's temporary. Think of yourself as an athlete who can benefit from learning. Take your next fall with style and grace. Bounce back. Move on.

DON'T QUIT

What stops success faster than failure? Quitting. And when do most people quit? When success is right around the corner. Failure will try to fool you and in some cunning way, try to undermine your determination. American inventor Thomas Alva Edison said, "Many of life's failures are people who did not realize how close they were to success when they gave up." Edison, like many great thinkers knew he would have more failures than success. But we don't think of him as a failure do we?

We can also see this in our country's fascination with institutions known as Halls of Fame. For instance, in the Rock and Roll Hall of Fame, nearly every musician honored has experienced more flops than hits. The same is true for heroes in The Baseball Hall of Fame, Cooperstown, NY. Visit it some day. You'll see that most of the record holders failed more than they succeeded. And that's the irony. We remember the successes. We forget the failures.

Do the same in your life. Remember the lesson—failure is there to teach. Learn from it. Move on. More than likely you'll have to fail your way to success. But you'll be in great company. That's the way the most renowned inventors changed the world, including Thomas Edison. He and his fellow inventors failed their way to success.

It has always been my belief that I rather give something a try and fail, than not even make an attempt. So embrace failure. Keep trying new things. If the attempts do not work out, fine. Learn from each and move onward.

> *"I was never afraid of failure, for I would sooner fail than not be among the best."*
>
> —John Keats

FAILURE ISN'T PERSONAL

Many people take failure as a personal shortcoming. Failure is a chance to learn and, as such, should not be taken personally. Failure just happens. In many cases, it can be an odd twist of circumstances. Other times, we see failure when it simply isn't there. This happens in downsizing. A person is laid off and may have a hard time finding a job. Does that mean the person is incompetent, unskilled and with no future? Of course not. Remember, employment and jobs are about business. Do not place business in the personal arena.

And remember that quote I asked you to copy at the beginning of this chapter in order to carry it with you? If you want to accelerate change as you head for success, begin each day by re-writing that very quote. Sorry: Xerox copying is not allowed. The hand must trace the words for the mind to embrace the truth. Here it is again, so worthy are the words of repetition:

"We are what we think. All that we are arises with our thought.

With our thoughts, we make our world."

—Buddha

And remember to learn from the animal kingdom, populated by noble beasts, large and small. While we all experience fear, face it head on. Know that both fear and mistakes are transitory. Be like an eagle. *Soar.*

"Half of the failures in life come from pulling one's horse when he is leaping."

—Thomas Hood

5

"It is the emotion which drives the intelligence forward in spite of obstacles."

—Henri Bergson

EMOTIONS

There's something fascinating about how top people seem to make the extremely difficult challenge appear easy. Two that have always stood out in my mind include Tiger Woods and Bruce Lee.

Tiger performs in such a consistent manner. He is near perfection no matter how taxing the challenge, or how difficult the terrain or how punishing the weather may be. The surrounding variables can be wildly different yet Tiger Woods remains consistent and constant.

Bruce Lee, too, continues to amaze me, certainly as a martial arts expert, but his words continue to resonate practically on a daily basis. This Bruce Lee quote is among my favorites: *Ever since I was a child I have had this instinctive urge for expansion and growth. To me, the function and duty of a quality human being is the sincere and honest development of one's potential.*

But there's something additional to the performances of Tiger Woods and Bruce Lee that sets each apart. Men and women who excel in their chosen fields, similar to Woods and Lee, quickly master maintaining emotional *control over the day-to-day challenges, especially when things go haywire.*

Handling emotions—yours and those of others—can be *the* decisive factor in many of life's pivotal moments. Appropriate emotional responses have the potential to really set you apart. Can you remain calm and seek the best solution? Or do your emotions tend to escalate rapidly? Are you useless when people experience rage? Do you tend to just sit there, feeling helpless, or worse—superior?

There is an undeniable freedom when one masters emotional responses. (Remember, fear is quite a different emotion, far more complex than the average day-to-day emotional range, so I address Effects of Fear in Chapter Four.) So while everyday emotions are different, how we respond can be as paralyzing as fear itself. It shouldn't be that way.

So how can you handle emotionally charged situations?

Some people pride themselves on their ability to simply walk away. Consistently walking out when things heat up, *and you're involved,* is not resolving the issue. It may appear to represent a more mature response. But in fact, it really isn't: One can't walk away from life's difficult situations time and time again and feel good, confident and in control. So learning how to cope and facilitate the solution is key.

Huang Po, a Chinese Zen Master, wrote:

"Do not permit the events of your daily lives to bind you, but never withdraw yourselves from them. Only by acting thus can you earn the title A Liberated One."

Here are 8 approaches that work for me.

COMPARTMENTALIZE

When a serious problem threatens a true professional, and others get swept up in the emotion of the crisis, a pro stays focused on finding a solution. No matter what else is happening to others, a top performer can effectively compartmentalize the problem and begin to resolve the predicament.

To contain the problem, these effective strategies seek positive solutions:

Isolate key issues.
Break down the problem and start to tick off possible ways to fix the situation.
Use logic to resolve *the situation.*
(See one caution below: Logic doesn't consistently work on people!)

Now, what do you do when *others* have been swept up into the rise of emotions?

CHOOSE YOUR BATTLES

When emotions flare, remember: Not everything is a crisis. Stress invariably magnifies reality. Learn to choose issues and identify those that are more critical than others.

STEER

No matter how desperate a situation appears to be, you still have choices. Circumstances often hijack emotions and people tend to follow their emotions. But you are fully able to steer yourself.

I often refer to this as a "redirect." How best to do it? Simply take a step aside and become open-minded. Let go of negative energy and simply redirect how you may choose to look at the situation. When you redirect your point of view you actually are steering yourself and your choices. Don't let the circumstances—or another person's reaction—dictate your emotional response. In this way you are able to effectively navigate through complex situations, often fraught with emotions.

LISTEN

Listen to feelings as well as to words when an issue begins to escalate. It sounds simple. But it's tough to do. At the slightest irritation, even the most stalwart types can revert to trigger reactions; they roll their eyes, sarcasm enters the conversation and quickly the situation unwinds.

"You cannot truly listen and do anything else at the same time."

—*M. Scott Peck*

REFLECTIVE LISTENING

This is a slightly different tool than just listening. But it is one of the most potent for resolving nearly any emotional situation. An agitated person, someone who is really, really upset or raging with anger, cannot be reeled back by *your* compartmentalizing *their* situation. It may seem trite, but most people—when they feel injured or slighted—*simply need someone else to listen.*

So yes, listen but also occasionally interrupt and play back what they are saying to you. It appears as if you are seeking clarification and perhaps you are. After all, emotionally charged minds tend to bounce around and not make a good deal of sense.

But playing back what the person is saying—reflective listening—brings them around very quickly. This does not mean you have to agree with what the person is saying or show sympathy, especially if you feel none is warranted. But you can be empathetic and listen, playing back key points as the person works through their emotions.

AVOID LOGIC

Remember that first tip about compartmentalizing? And how well logic works when you feel overwhelmed by emotions during a crisis? Guess what? It doesn't work the other way around. And it hardly ever works on people. When someone else is upset, the last thing you need to employ in their presence is logic. That's because logic simply cannot effectively read the full emotional range of a person. In fact, to some people who are experiencing an emotional reaction, logic gives the impression that you are dismissing their reaction. That's because logic ignores emotion—and using it often equates to your suggesting they're wrong to feel the way they do. Logic frustrates people even more when they're emotional. You need not engage in their plight and encourage their tailspin. You can stay neutral and calm. Just don't tell them logically what you think they should do. Most people who are upset are not looking for logical answers.

> *"Feelings are not supposed to be logical; dangerous is the man who has rationalized his emotions."*
>
> —David Borenstein

EMPATHY

Learn how to gauge a situation through another person's eyes and heart, whether you agree with that person or not. Empathy is the ability to be so secure in your own thoughts, feelings, and values that you can also perceive opposing points of view without getting emotional and exasperated. There's a meaningful side benefit to genuine empathy, especially in the work force. If you're an empathetic colleague or boss, people generally feel more loyalty to, and are willing to go that extra mile for those who somehow "tune in to them."

Rein It In

Some people feel showing a steely calm, acting the stoic, makes them more effective. I'm not sure true stoics consistently rise to the top because somehow they seem to lack a certain humanity, don't they? Have you ever noticed how world leaders can quickly age during tenure or office? I'm sure that's because all leaders, like the rest of the world, experience the most difficult of feelings, including toxic stress and anger, even grief—though their stress is on a more continual basis and collapsed into a few years.

I'm sure every top CEO (and nearly every world class athlete I know), at one time or another, felt like pulling an over-the-top tantrum. But not all do. The real pros rein it in. It doesn't mean they don't feel a wide range of emotions. They do. They just know how to reasonably contain their emotional displays. In some ways, they typify a great quote of Confucius, *"When anger rises, think of the consequences."*

"If you can imagine it, you can achieve it; if you can dream it, you can become it."

—William Arthur Ward

6

"*Coming together is a beginning.*
Keeping together is progress.
Working together is success. "

—*Henry Ford*

INTERPERSONAL
SKILLS

THE FINE ART OF BEING
A PEOPLE PERSON

No matter how hard you work or how brilliant your ideas, if you're unable to successfully connect with people, especially those who work around you, your professional life will derail or chug to a halt. Even telecommuters must have great interpersonal skills, though they may rely mostly on email or the telephone. If you can't relate to those around you, even though you may earn millions and win hundreds of awards, then on some level you have failed.

In coaching, I've witnessed a few really smart people completely caught off guard to learn a "guaranteed promotion" will not be forthcoming. Why? They just don't seem to be able to motivate people, or they fail to get along with others. Several are surprised to learn they lack finesse. After all, they get right to the point, what's wrong with that? Their clueless attitude rarely asks for feedback. They see the world only through *their* personal prism. They tend to be smart, even brilliant, and at the head of their class as far as skill sets are concerned.

Increasingly innovative companies are selecting top candidates based on how well that person relates to colleagues, friends, even strangers. That's what drives the final decision.

If you've participated in a job interview for a coveted slot and have been asked about an improbable scenario—or how you might handle a hypothetical hurdle—this likely is a screening tool to test aspects of your empathy, attitude and flexibility. Employers know they can pretty much teach smart people many of the on-the-job skills to deliver an outstanding performance. But when a person's high productivity comes at the expense of the well being of others, that exceptional performance loses value.

I believe practically all of us can improve in the interpersonal skill area. We get lazy because we often feel pressed for time. When we're busy, we don't take time for others. Our communication takes a short form. Inevitably we use an unnecessarily curt response. We grow impatient when others miss what we view to be the very obvious solution to a given challenge. Tempers flare.

But minor stressors don't seem to plague true leaders. That's because remarkable leaders have a whole arsenal of useful tools to get good work out of people while making those very same people feel valued and important. Especially when the heat is turned up.

In order to strengthen interpersonal skills, we all need to be honest with our own failings. It's our shortcomings that trip us up, not the actions of others.

Let me encourage you to remain fluid throughout this process. Don't be rigid. Be honest about your interaction with everyone. The cashier, airline ticket agent, family members and coworkers. Everyone. Watch the full range of responses for an entire week. Expect human errors, not perfection. And observe how you react. Do you seek to win each point? Do you fail to give credit to others? Are you the one who corrects others? When someone appears upset, do you dismiss their reaction as foolish? Keep an open mind. Open your heart to humanity. And remember: Even when others are wrong, it's up to you to work around the hurdle successfully. Avoid the blame game.

BE AN APPRECIATOR

It may sound simplistic, but great leaders generally appreciate life and people. Praising others is an integral component of those who have great personal style. Kind words cost you nothing yet an honest compliment can be priceless and endure as an important memory for a very long time. Recognition is the greatest motivator because it permits the person to feel valued. This is especially true when the pressure mounts to complete an urgent project. To be an authentic appreciator, look for value where others see shortcomings.

Help others to fulfill their need to feel valued. Use appreciation and positive reinforcement as the two most powerful building blocks to help in any learning situation. Good performance is everywhere; begin to notice it. Another simple tip is to simply remove the word "should" from your vocabulary. When seeking to help another colleague, even though we may be well intentioned and caring, the use of the word "should"—especially when we offer advice—adopts a toxic tone. "You *should* do it this way. You really *should* ask first." We may wish to be helpful by offering tips but when our advice is laced with a litany of "shoulds," our suggestions come across as downright bossy.

We've all worked with a negative thinker, the gloomy naysayer of life. There are few things worse than a chronic complainer or whiner. Don't be one. If you must verbalize a grievance, vent to one friend who knows you well—not a group who will likely feed the grievance. Say what is bothering you. Keep it short. Process the grievance. Move on. Spare those around you.

Another small thing we tend to forget is simply saying thank you. Do it more often. Make colleagues feel welcome when they call or stop by your office. If you let others know that they are appreciated, they'll want to give you their best.

ONLY NEGOTIATE WIN-WIN DEALS

Negotiation is not a competition to beat the other person. That's the ego at work. When it comes to making deals and securing agreements, use your brain but also use heart and spirit. Don't let your ego drive the bargain or engage in a battle of wills. Any deal you construct must benefit all parties. The unwritten rule of negotiation is to conduct business in a straightforward fashion and to "do the right thing." If the deal falls through, be able to walk away with your self-respect.

YOUR INNER WORLD REFLECTS YOUR OUTER WORLD

It's a well-known law of the universe: Feeling successful will attract more success. If you feel inferior inside or continue to long for things that are missing in your life, that's what the universe will send your way. The more you long for happiness, the less it will come your way. The poorer you feel and the more you want to be rich, the poorer you will stay. Truly magnanimous workers end up achieving more in life and reaping greater rewards simply because they know that their inner world determines their outer world. They feel good about themselves and life, even when things turn upside down. They don't panic when things go awry. They don't whine and complain when life presents tough challenges. It may sound ironic, even impossible to understand, but when life delivers challenging blows to great people, most hold on to a bit of inner peace throughout the chaos. They know setbacks are temporary. They are content to know who they are and they feel that personal sense of goodness inside. In order to attract fulfillment and success and live with daily happiness, you must *first become these very things.*

BUILD AN EMOTIONAL TEAM

Never push yourself toward burnout. The brain, heart and soul shut down when stress and strain become too much to bear. The best way to avoid burnout is to learn to rely on a hand-picked emotional team that has your best interest at heart. When things get dicey, some feel compelled to go it alone. Don't! We all need an emotional team to help us sort through challenges. The team's perspective may be more accurate than any conclusions you try to develop on your own. Don't be so self-sufficient that you withdraw and let pride dictate that you 'go it alone.' The best athletes have coaches. Many of them have several coaches at one time. Top executives, too, know to develop a support team, upon whom they may rely unconditionally. Choose 'team members' who are intelligent and resourceful so that creating new and innovative solutions are second nature. When life is at its best, it's amazing how many people are willing to come along and enjoy the ride. But when things trend downward, that's when you may need *true* friends to help navigate the bumps in the road. Be prepared to ask for help.

BE SELF-RELIANT

This may appear to contradict the above point. It doesn't. Succeeding in martial arts is traceable to a person's ability to achieve *balance*. For the most part, you must rely more on yourself than on others. Take responsibility for your success. And take responsibility for your failures. When I stress self-reliance, I am urging people to look inward for happiness, not outward. Don't look to others for validation. Don't look to others for happiness. Seeking success inside is the definition of self-reliance. It means you follow your own path, to be sure. And the balance comes when you walk your own path, but never to the exclusion of the outside world.

SMILE

Yes, I know it sounds "out there". Yet it's true. We'd all rather work with someone who is happy and pleasant to be around, not a whiner or complainer. Maintain a positive, cheerful attitude about work and about life. The positive energy you radiate will draw others to you. Smile.

REVENGE HAS NO POSITIVE VALUE

Seeking to even the score will take its toll on *you*. Revenge is a terrible energy. It will eat you up faster than it will destroy the other party. Revenge will poison *you* more. Don't goad others. Don't seek revenge. I know it sounds too facile, even impossible, to move to the 'higher ground' when you feel a terrible misdeed has been aimed at you. But I have to be clear: Let go of anger. Put it behind you. Move on.

NOTICE YOUR COLLEAGUES

For the most part, American companies feature informal work environments. Address people by their first names. And use their names in conversations. If you're not great with remembering names, then find a clever way to carve them into your memory. Make eye contact. Pay attention to what's going on in other people's lives. Acknowledge their happy milestones, and express concern and sympathy for difficult situations. Empathy is an art. Find the right balance. Don't be a loner. Engage colleagues and solicit the opinions of others.

LISTEN ACTIVELY

If I could encourage you to adopt one single communication trait that will serve you well throughout your life, it's this: *Seek to understand the other person's point of view.* The best way? Be quiet and listen. Obvious, right? Try it the next time someone comes to you—how good a listener are you?

Most people fail in this area simply because they tend to interrupt or *glean for facts.* The latter—listening only for facts—tends to eliminate the human element and that's when communication can deteriorate. Try to understand what the other person is seeking to say. Watch the non-verbal cues. Be sensitive. It neither means you have to agree with the person nor share his point of view. But it does mean you may have to remove the filters that make the message either right or wrong in your mind. Good listeners seek to understand and minimize judgmental calls.

The best way to facilitate listening when a situation presents an emotional challenge is to restate what you think the person is saying, using your own words to paraphrase the situation. Failed politicians and ousted corporate honchos typically are the ones who simply *did not hear what their constituency or shareholders sought to communicate.* They didn't listen.

BE A FACILITATOR. DON'T BE DIVISIVE.

Bring people together. Appreciators are also keen facilitators. Treat everyone equally, and don't play favorites. Avoid talking about others behind their backs. I have a simple rule: If I'm not going to say something to a person directly, then I'm not going to say it to someone else. Petty comments; laughing at someone else's expense, is mean-spirited, unattractive and small-minded—typical behavior of those who feel the need for silly power-based cliques. It's divisive and the polar opposite of being a facilitator. You can only gain trust when your colleagues identify you as someone they can rely upon. When they see you are fair and solid, true loyalty emerges and makes for a productive team.

CHOOSE YOUR BATTLES

There are times when people need to find their own resolutions. You can't solve the world's problems. But all true leaders are effective mediators; they don't step away from disputes simply because the situation may be heated. Find a way to sit down with both sides and help sort out differences. Permitting sniping to continue and ignoring a grievance—whether it is real or imagined—is what drives dysfunction.

The best mediators are able to see two sides of a dispute and resolve a conflict so both sides feel they have been treated equitably. This is the true strength of empathy—seeing two opposing sides and bringing about a fair resolution so hard feelings evaporate. To do this well, you also must be in touch with your own emotions. Don't suppress feelings. Feel them; identify them accurately. And do the same for those around you. Out of this process, comes empathy.

> "The greatest compliment that was ever paid to me was when someone asked me what I thought, and attended to my answer."
>
> —Henry David Thoreau

7

"A leader needs enough understanding to fashion an intelligent strategy."

—John Kotter

PRODUCTIVITY TOOLS

All of us must remain flexible to grow. And yet we all are often required increasingly to handle vast amounts of ever-changing information, all dispatched at speedy rates. Nearly every profession has a set of tools that help get the job done. A computer technician may have a variety of software programs to fix an infected hard drive and a writer may consider words effective "tools of the trade" to clearly communicate ideas.

For this reason, I feel practically everyone needs a collection of productivity tools—simple ways to stay mentally organized. *Without being mentally organized, it's impossible to achieve goals.* Sounds simplistic, I'm sure. But it has proven true for me. And it has proven true for countless top martial arts clients as well. No one can achieve any degree of martial arts expertise without experiencing mental organization. It's the power that permits a person to break through barriers. Here are some ideas I use to stay prepared.

KILL CLUTTER

Your desk is a mirror of you. Dump the junk. Wherever you work, whatever your job, free up your surface space. When in doubt; throw out. Have a dedicated basket for pending projects; stack according to deadline. Be able to reach for anything that needs immediate attention. Get rid of broken equipment, triage clutter, have adequate shelving. And all of that incoming mail? Become as paperless as possible. Read and toss.

USE A DAILY PLANNER

Eliminate notes and Post It® reminders. Appointments and commitments need to be recorded consistently and *only in one place*. Buy a good planner. Most large office supply outlets carry several types. Some people prefer electronic organizers. You may have to shop around to find the right planner that works for you. But you need one. And you must be able to put your hands on it readily at all times.

A Planner is Not a Calendar

Make your planner work hard; it's not just a calendar. Use it to record goals on a time line. Nearly every top performer I have coached often spends more time *planning* than actually doing. *Planning equates to seizing control of your life*. If you work an average seven- or eight-hour day, then set aside a minimum of one hour daily exclusively for planning. This is not about managing your calendar. It's different: it's about planning important goals, assigning due dates and making things happen.

Back Up

Make sure your data is backed up regularly, including address books, even personal photos. Automate the process. Use external drives and take the data off site.

Plan The Day Before

Setting aside a specific and consistent time to plan makes a big difference. Most people arrive at work, sip their morning coffee and outline a To Do list.

I think this is a mistake.

Do your planning the night before. It will make a supreme difference. Before you shut down the computer (or whatever you do that signals the end of the day), wrap your head around tomorrow and the next few days and use your planner: What needs immediate attention in the coming days? What project might wait a day until you have everyone's signature? In sum, put first things first. Look ahead to the next month, too.

By planning the night before, you wake up knowing where you are headed and what your top priorities are. Also, when you need to make modifications and changes, the distance of planning the night before lends a meaningful perspective. One tends to visualize more efficient solutions and inevitable changes are less frustrating.

THE IMPOSSIBLE

Every now and again, an unwieldy assignment arrives at a time when you can't quite handle it. You feel overwhelmed. But handle it you must. So how to tackle the impossible?

Easy. Break the project down into smaller tasks. List the three key phases from beginning to middle to end. You can use index cards and tape them to a wall if that helps you see the overall project. Then break each of these three phases down into smaller units. Next, estimate the time to do each of these phases—if you're unsure of how to estimate time, then continue to break down that particular phase into even smaller steps and guesstimate the time for each step. Plot the complete timeline out on one sheet of paper. Recognize that some unknown variables may pull the project off schedule—people are on vacation and can't get back to you, that sort of thing. Attach a slide factor for each phase.

As the project takes off, you will be wise to review the time line, evaluate the progress and make adjustments. Don't carry all of the variable parts of an impossible challenge in your head!

Don't like planning? You're more of a do-ER? Well think about this: A personal crisis or midlife meltdown occurs when a perfectly fine person wakes up one day, perspiring madly simply because he or she is not even close to fulfilling a dream. Time is passing them by. They awaken to discover the dreams they felt were guaranteed in their youth are no closer than they were decades ago. Plan. It is never too late to make your lot in life better.

MEMORY

There's a lot of new information that explains how the brain functions. In the last half of the 20th century, medical science researched the human body seemingly at the expense of understanding how the brain works. Now, thankfully, that gap in understanding has narrowed.

Some people focus better, others have huge attention deficits. Work styles reflect how a person thinks and processes information. Other influences such as chemotherapy, stroke, depression, brain injury, medication, even hormonal changes can create cognitive impairment, either temporarily or long term.

But even perfectly healthy people, often in their prime, may feel their memory is not as sharp as it once was. Honestly, I think we tend to exaggerate our memory shortfall.

For instance, short-term memory is not truly geared to store important information. (That's why it's called short-term memory!). Short-term memory receives day-to-day information that washes over all of us. Unless we seek to store what we *need to know* in our *long-term* memory, the *short-term* memory simply discards the information.

If you're healthy but find yourself feeling scattered, try these simple memory tips.

- *Rip Up Notes.* When I was in my twenties, I would attend an important lecture and take notes. What used to drive my colleagues crazy is that I'd stand up after the lecture and rip up my notes. Eventually they figured out my methodology: writing down key facts helped move important information into my long-term memory. I didn't need the notes.

Simply writing down a few key words reinforced my retention of this information. Of course you can't mindlessly take notes—you have to concentrate on the information.

+ *Don't Multi-Task.* Doing several things at one time is the bane of our modern lives. If something requires your consideration, give it your undivided attention. Don't multi task when your attention needs to be focused on something important.

+ *Scan. Underline. Review.* A report arrives on your desk and it needs your attention. As you scan it—or read carefully—underline only those key points you'll need to retain later on. When you're done, once again review—without interruption—those key points. This initiates what I call long-term memory retrieval. You'll need to concentrate a bit on those key points. But not for long; spend a few minutes only. Then put the information aside. To prevent the information from being discarded by your short-term memory, review the key facts again, perhaps no later than the next day. Spend three minutes. Keep scanning these key facts at regular, short intervals, though allowing more time in between each mini review session. Research indicates that the mind only needs an occasional "booster review" in order to place the data in long-term memory.

ROLE MODEL

Use the behavior and strategies of other peak performers to accelerate your own path. Identify others who have achieved what you want—or who have mastered a certain skill—and cultivate their approach. Role models show us it can be done and *how* to do it.

Mentors

Enlisting someone capable who is able to guide you and *willingly* show you the ropes— can accelerate your own personal journey. A good mentor will offer constructive ways to perfect mental organization. Adapt the tips to your own style and make them work. You, too, can simultaneously offer to mentor someone who needs to move up the ladder. Make personal growth about give and take.

Manage Minutes

I don't promote micromanaging but there are some tasks that you can take care of in two minutes or less. When you come across them, attend to them. File that one folder instead of stacking up files throughout the day and having to reshuffle a dozen or so at the end of the day when you're less sharp.

Feel Good

With few exceptions, the foundation of good health rests with you. You can monitor your diet, develop an exercise routine, maintain a healthy lifestyle and manage your weight.

If you're out of shape, you just don't feel good about yourself. Then confidence drops. Energy dissipates. You experience dissatisfaction. You under-perform. Anger may percolate. Seize control and take responsibility. And I'll remind you again: Standing straight and good posture generate positive energy.

THE POWER OF NO

Seeking to do a job while being a slave to the opinions of others works against you. It will weaken your performance. Don't be a constant approval seeker. Get comfortable saying no. Accepting additional projects when you are already committed to pressing deadlines shows a lack of personal respect. Doing favors when you have no free time or trying to always accommodate the various burdens that hit each day, are self-sabotage. Know time is one of your most valuable resources. Learn to say no.

PERSONAL DEVELOPMENT

Personal development is about finding passion. It's about enhancing performance. Discovering what you're truly good at—not what your family, educators or friends say you do best—requires introspection over time. Yet, unbelievably, a very small percent of the population, some estimate only 5% or less, ever takes a serious whack at exploring personal development.

Explore creative ways to unleash your talents and grow. Try out different techniques; explore big or small strategies that promote self-discovery. Never stop learning. Self-education can make you a fortune. But self-discovery will deliver riches that can't be measured.

WOULD I HIRE ME?

Who doesn't occasionally gripe about something? It's part of human nature. But who among ourselves takes time to scrutinize our performance and ask the obvious question, "Would I hire me?" Every now and then take a hard look at your performance. Evaluate your output objectively. Ask the questions a reasonable boss or employer might. And answer honestly.

SELF-REWARDS

Use rewards to create a continual motivation. Don't wait for something major to occur. Treat yourself well and reward your efforts on a daily basis.

UNDERSTAND PROFIT

Get comfortable with the concept of profitability. Without profits, there is no business. Profits need not be won on the backs of those who are less fortunate. And profits give each of us—corporations included—the ability to make financial contributions to a world in need. Again, it's a question of balance.

BE SENSITIVE TO TIME

There are times when a sense of urgency is needed. We all know what a true emergency is. But are you the one who tries to get everything done—say right before a long-planned vacation, when these tasks could have been addressed earlier? Unnecessary urgency is a terrible use of energy. It shows little respect for time. Time is a commodity. It is to be revered and respected; eventually it will run out. Be sensitive to it.

OHIO

Only Handle It Once—OHIO—is generally a good rule. It certainly applies to all junk mail and also the bulk of mindless email that inundate our days. Shuffling papers back and forth, scrolling through emails, thinking, "I'll get to that later," is just a waste of time. Set aside time to deal with email—you need not wrestle with email throughout your day. And not every email or piece of paper that hits your desk requires a response.

Phone Log

I receive a lot of phone calls. And I have to place a lot of calls, too. When the incoming and outgoing messages stack up and relate to critically important projects with specific due dates, create a one-sheet phone log: Enter the person's name, number, message and call status. If you find yourself repeatedly looking for telephone numbers or wondering if that person returned your call—or did you call them back?—a phone log can keep you mentally organized.

"What do you want to achieve or avoid? The answers to this question are objectives. How will you go about achieving your desired results?

The answer to this you can call strategy."

—William E. Rothschild

8

"One of the symptoms of an approaching nervous breakdown is the belief that one's work is terribly important."

—Bertrand Russell

BALANCE

THE ART OF BALANCE

"Work is a means of living, it is not life itself"

—*Mahatma Gandhi.*

I really enjoy re-visiting this quote. It identifies a value that is among the worthiest: balance. Without balance we compromise our purpose, general happiness and eventually it takes its toll in all areas, including health.

When any of us places greater emphasis on one aspect of life, *to the exclusion of other equally important aspects*, then we miss the point of living. We diminish our chance of achieving self-fulfillment. A job is not life itself. For example, building great personal wealth at the expense of a being a loving, supporting friend, colleague or spouse—or at the expense of becoming a great parent to a child—

makes the wealth hallow, devoid of true value. It imbues one's life with emptiness.

Without balance, we become hostage to extremes: We become either scattered or narrow in our thinking, either lethargic or overwrought in our energy, and either obsessed or depressed in approach to life. Invariably our health and our well-being, and our relationship with those for whom we care, are collectively jeopardized.

So what is balance anyway? For me, balance combines two important components: achievement and enjoyment. Balance percolates to the surface when we experience a meaningful sense of achievement, coupled with enjoyment. And these two components must exist together across the important realms of work, family/friends/self.

Your personal sense of balance, like my personal sense of balance, is in constant flux. Most likely yours—and mine—will continually vary over time. The right balance during your first job, perhaps as a single person immediately after college, will be quite different than when you marry. The right balance for you today may be remarkably different than the balance you may require tomorrow.

Truthfully, there is no perfect, one-size-fits-all recipe for balance. Balance cannot be put on autopilot so that you easily sail through each day. That's because you live with certain priorities today that likely will change overnight.

An interesting psychological twist suggests that people whose lives are out of balance, often don't even recognize the disparity. Why? They lack the ability to step back and view the situation from a variety of angles. A lack of perspective contributes to imbalance. An inability to take inventory of important personal values invariably places a life out of balance. Here are some signs that your life may suffer from a lack of equilibrium:

You bring work home with you.

You've missed important personal events—a child's birthday or a family reunion.

You roll over vacation time and take no personal days.

Monday rolls around and you feel exhausted.

You can't recall the last time you read a book, simply for pleasure.

You don't have time for your hobbies and other fun activities.

You rarely go to a movie, play or visit a museum.

You rarely enjoy downtime before the next project hits.

Your schedule is packed—practically every hour is planned.

You've lost sight of who you are.

You can't quite recall why you chose this career path; your job has lost meaning.

So many people, family and friends depend on you.

I learned some valuable lessons when I set my sights on claiming the World Record title. I learned to ask myself three key questions on a daily basis.

I call them The Three G's of life: Give, Grow and Gratitude.

Ask yourself these questions on a daily basis.

1: What do I have to **give** to life and the world around me?

Try to determine what *your special* talents are. The more awareness you develop about your own gifts, the more you are able to spread these talents to the world at large. It can be as simple as discovering you're a "people person." If that's true, you'll soon notice that your everyday exchanges with perfect strangers have a way of lifting their spirit. Believe me, that's no small contribution to humanity. (Imagine a world where everyone was kind to strangers.) When your talents are offered to the world at large, you'll soon discover that this form of giving triggers the other Two G's.

2: How am I looking to **grow** in life?

No matter how insignificant you imagine your talent to be, if you give it value, invariably talent seeks to grow. So now ask, "How do I hope to grow?" Identify other talents you hope to cultivate. Ask, "Am I headed in the direction that will promote self-discovery and growth?"

Will this growth make you a better person so you may continue to honor the first "G", to give? Invariably, by recognizing your talents and placing yourself on a path of growth, the third "G", feeling grateful begins to trickle into your daily life.

3: What am I **GRATEFUL** for?

Balance is impossible to achieve without feeling grateful about something, anything.

Bitterness, anger and any negative emotion instantly throw a person out of kilter. Conversely, the best conduit for balance is experiencing a sense of gratitude; especially when one also may be facing great stress, say from the loss of a job.

How can any of us move on to what we want if we are not grateful in the present moment for what we have? Feeling grateful is the underlying force that guides the law of attraction. It may be difficult to see at times, but your life—everyone's life—offers much.

Life is filled with opportunities. Opportunities can be small. Or they can be large. Sometimes opportunities may be invisible; you have to search for them. But if you can feel grateful about certain aspects of your life, watch reciprocity kicks in. And as you feel grateful and enjoy your new sense of balance, guess what? Invariably you want to give something to the world around you. Without missing a beat, you circle back to the first "G." When you're grateful, you wish to share the goodness. And so it goes. The three G's are an intriguing loop, all interconnected as a single path and one that is worth circling back to, throughout your day, as you enjoy a new sense of balance.

12 Strategies for Balance

Let me share a dozen personal strategies, all easy to implement strategies, which can make a big difference in creating flow and balance. They work for me.

1 - Truth

We throw our lives out of balance when we begin to pursue paths that have no value for us. Is it as simple as that? Yes. We leave our inspiring beliefs and values behind and chug off in the wrong direction. Our days no longer reflect our personal truth. Wham: Within a short period of time, life is out of whack.

So ask yourself: What do you believe? And how does your performance match these beliefs? Get clear on what you want.

And while life often is about some compromise, when we consistently jeopardize those values that have the most meaning for each of us personally, and do so on a daily basis, we throw our lives out of balance. If you are not truthful about seeking the right path for you, I believe your life is out of balance.

2 - Bounce Back Time

Athletes are often pushed past the point of extreme pain simply to see what their capacity is. Unless you are an athlete about ready to turn pro, this approach makes no sense whatsoever. It produces burnout. Guess what? Most workers do not recover from job burnout. It creates the end of the road and is a wasteful approach to seeking better productivity.

Understand the value of recoup time and protect it with a vengeance. Recovery, or what I call bounce-back time, is a way to renew life. Recovery time permits each of us an opportunity to repair our bodies, keep our psyches resilient and conserve our valuable energy output.

Most people blame a bad job or a too-demanding boss for job burnout. But avoiding burnout is a personal responsibility. Do not ever place yourself in harm's way.

Know when you are approaching phases that become too burdensome, and build in bounce-back time. It can be amazingly easy to do: set aside an evening or afternoon for simple recreation. Take the phone off the hook, shut down the computer and try different activities, especially those you can do with others. Let your mind grow quiet. Bounce back time shows a necessary respect for both mental and physical cycles.

And, as an aside, get enough sleep and protect your immune system. You can't bounce back when you are sleep-deprived or weakened by a cold. Besides, sleep deprivation creates costly mistakes, another time waster that gets you off track and creates imbalance. Do it right the first time.

3 - REFLECTION VIA A SABBATICAL

Having purpose and knowing where you want to go, as outlined in the Chapter Nine relating to goals, is only one path to creating success. I urge you to take a sabbatical, create a planned break, and visit a tranquil and beautiful place of nature in order to simply reflect. We don't do enough of this in our western world. A life that is not examined is not worth living.

Plan time by yourself. Do it *for* you. This is a constructive way to heighten your imagination. Allow solitude to enter your day. Reflection is as important as having a vision. It also feeds balance.

4 - CURIOSITY

Remain interested in the world around you. Creative and curious people are open to possibilities and this alone helps generate balance. Avoid being convinced that your way is *the* only way—be willing to suspend belief and stay open. Be a lifetime learner.

And a note about the ego: Often our wounded ego rises up to kill different approaches, or squelch innovative thinking. It's our tired soul that suggests, "It can't be done. We tried that already." If you're in a "been there, done that" mode, allow balance to enter your life via a sabbatical.

People with specialized interests often pursue these hobbies at the expense of social interaction. But this, too, is limiting. Don't be a loner. Don't hibernate.

5 - LAUGH

Without balance comes stress. Stress eventually makes a person jaded, even humorless. The most potent antidote to stress is humor. How lighthearted is your outlook? Are you laughing and enjoying life? If you're devoid of humor and laughter as you move through your day, something major is likely out of balance. Yes, there are some people—notably certain types of doctors and those who deal with disaster relief, who cannot laugh as they seek to solve major problems. Still, the best of these know the value of instilling joy and laughter *off the job*.

Humor offers a fresh perspective and permit balance to return. You know what to do: offset pressure by exploring past times that make you laugh. Start hanging out with happier people, too! Find joy in life.

6 - Be Present

Peace comes from acceptance. We all may have things we chose to change and areas we wish to improve. We seek these improvements as a means to align our life with meaning. Still, I urge you to adopt a paradox of sorts: Accept who you are now. Accept the "here and now" and seek peace today. Be comfortable with yourself now.

The only thing you truly own or have is the present time. Celebrate it. Enjoy the supreme sense of balance that being present creates. Be at peace with yourself.

7 - Leave Work *There*

Leave office projects at the office. Today's work environment permits each of us to connect with anyone at any time from virtually anywhere. Since there is little boundary between work and home, it's up to you to create it. Make a conscious decision to separate and protect your personal time. Turn off your cell phone. Do not respond to email—and let people know ahead of time, that you intend to stay offline. Stay away from the computer.

8 - Keep a Log

What robs you of equilibrium? What is it? If you honestly can't identify why your life feels rocky, then you likely have distanced yourself *too far* from those things that give you joy. More than likely you may have eliminated the things you value from your day-to-day existence.

I'm often surprised to learn some clients haven't a clue as to why their days seem out of balance. After discussion I learn that the person has placed too great a distance between having joy and doing a good job. In a sense, the person is completely disconnected from living the good life.

Awareness helps the person re-connect to what has meaning and the quickest way to accomplish this is by beginning an informal log. If you feel this may be an issue for you, then I urge you to become more aware of your emotional reaction as you move through the day. Begin to circle those things that pull you away from happiness and do not reflect your values. Cut out or delegate a number of activities you don't enjoy *and don't have time for.* Decide what is critically important.

9 - FLEXIBILITY AND OPTIONS

Take advantage of possible choices that you previously may have eschewed as not "you." Most people who focus exclusively on work alone pay a terrible price at some point in their life. Are you one of those people? To establish balance, seek ways in your current employment situation to introduce flexibility. Does your employer offers flex hours? Can you work a different, even compressed workweek? How about telecommuting? Options must be explored as a means to avoid the rigidity that is throwing your life out of balance.

10 - DECLINE

You've read it elsewhere: *No* is a word that can actually empower you. Saying "No" helps re-introduce balance. When you quit doing things out of a false sense of obligation, you'll make more room in your life for the activities that are meaningful and bring joy. Saying "No" can elevate your stock among peers and others. Learn to decline invitations and say no to spearheading new projects. Take a breather.

11 - CREATE BALANCE

It is up to you to instill balance. No one else can do it so own it! Bolster your support system. Give yourself the gift of a trusted buddy or supportive colleague who you can turn to and discuss options during times of stress or hardship. Ensure you have trusted friends and relatives who can assist you when you need to work overtime or travel for your job. These helpful colleagues and friends are not in your life to hear you whine. Make the interaction positive as you earnestly seek ways to restore balance into your day.

12 - Time Management

If you have tried to create balance before, only to fail several times, may I make a simple suggestion? Now may be the time to spend some money and get professional help via a proven and effective time-management seminar. There are a variety of solid conferences offered on a national level as well as a variety of classic books published on time management. Begin to check out what is offered and find a program that adapts to your style. I found Franklin Covey offers a great time-management workshop utilizing their daily planner and it made a difference in my being able to create balance.

"The best and safest thing is to keep balance in your life, acknowledge the great powers around us and in us. If you can do that, and live that way, you are a really wise man."

—Euripides

9

"Goals help focus you on areas in both your personal and professional life that are important and meaningful, rather than being guided by what other people want you to be, do, or accomplish."

—Catherine Pulsifer

GOALS

On pages 123 through 131, you'll find your workbook for Breaking Through Barriers.

As a coach and a martial arts follower, I believe in the possibilities of each individual. Yes, you can achieve your dreams and make goals a reality. One has to begin somewhere. And as Thomas Henry Huxley wrote, *"The rung of the ladder was never meant to rest upon, but only to hold a man's foot long enough to enable him to put the other somewhat higher."*

So let's get to it.

Your Internal Compass

The first section explains an inner dynamic I describe as an Internal Compass. Everyone has an Internal Compass. However, understanding the power of an Internal Compass helps a person understand why a person's beliefs often dictate choices. You'll learn how your Internal Compass dictates your general mood and everyday feelings. If you're off course, or if you have the sense that you'll never be able to achieve your dreams, that's because your Internal Compass somehow points you towards failure.

Awareness is key to finding balance. Learn how to re-set your Internal Compass so you can point yourself in the right direction.

The Simple Art of Self-Discipline

Adopting self-discipline can be complex or easy. The choice is yours. Why not make it easy? Here's a way to get started.

How to Embark on Your Personal Breaking Barriers Action Plan

All you need is a simple spiral notebook and a pen or pencil to launch your final phase of your individual Breaking Barriers Action Plan.

I suggest most people take enough time to do the thinking and creating an action plan. For some it can be a few hours (or perhaps much more) allocated over several days. Give yourself enough time to make it work. Still, I find those clients who have the greatest success are the ones who remove all interruptions from the process so they can complete this final section in one shot. Many actually set aside a weekend devoted to establishing the correct action plan.

Again: It's a choice. Choose what works for you.

Ready? Let's get to it.

YOUR INTERNAL COMPASS

Values drive the behavior that helps a person achieve a goal.

Values are exceedingly powerful. Yet most of us are only vaguely aware of values and beliefs. So what are values anyway?

Values are a collection of beliefs that guide each of us in order to interface with the world.

In the simplest terms:

> *Your values either work on your behalf and make you stronger.*

> *Or*

> *Your values work against you through self-limiting beliefs that push success beyond your reach.*

Values set your Internal Compass in motion so that it guides personal conduct, establishes how you interact with others. It even helps shape career choices.

There are all sorts of ways to sum up the various value categories that make our Internal Compass work. I tend to lump values into four general categories, which I'll share with you. The four categories, which have considerable overlap, are:

- Personal Values
- Cultural Values
- Social Values
- Work Values

Personal Values. Personal values define you in the most intimate and specific terms. They make you unique. For example, those who endured hunger as youngsters may never quite sublimate their beliefs about deprivation. In some cases this can be a positive force, bringing about great personal success; in others it may drive negative behavior, such as overeating or excessive hoarding. Personal values are most directly linked to health, physical, family, home life and financial issues. And most of these values we adopt in our childhood, accepting as truth what parents, teachers and other adults teach us. As we mature, our spiritual and ethical beliefs become more sharply defined. In fact, the classic struggle experienced by many people seeking a fuller life can be traced to letting go of self-limiting beliefs that don't reflect their greater destiny.

Cultural Values. While personal values make us unique, often they bring us closer with others who share these same values. Cultural values connect us with our roots; they help individual people feel connected to a larger community with similar beliefs, values and backgrounds.

Social Values. This set of beliefs tend to define how an individual interfaces with other people, not just friends and family, but strangers or co-workers. Have you ever noticed how some people seem to sail through airport delays, mistakes on credit card charges, traffic snarls and other daily snags without so much as a sigh? That's because on some level their belief—or value—is that life is often colored by the unexpected, which often can be traced to simple human error. They don't take daily mishaps personally. Their social values urge them to grease the wheel of life, rather than create more conflict.

Work Values. These values guide how one makes a living, becomes financially productive and secure. While money and wealth are fraught with emotions and thus tend to reflect personal beliefs, work values are slightly different in that they reveal how you interface with those who may control an aspect of your destiny—say a superior, an immediate boss or those upon whom your success may rely, such as a client. Work values often reveal your potential for advancement within a structured environment such as a large corporation. And like all values we embrace, work values intersect with the three other areas that include personal, cultural and social values.

> You must know your values for what they are: Beliefs. Be able to wrestle with self-limiting beliefs in order to design a successful goal program.

FINGERPRINTS

Your values are exactly like fingerprints the world over—no two sets are alike. You may share certain beliefs with family members and close friends, but the deeper you explore personal beliefs, the more you are likely to see distinctions that define you alone. Values mark you choice of friends, how you handle money, how you perform at work and how you behave behind a wheel.

Self-limiting beliefs, your values exclusively, prevent you from achieving goals. Self-limiting beliefs, too, tend to drive pessimistic thinking and behavior. It's true: Optimists are more likely to achieve goals.

VALUES DICTATE HOW YOU FEEL DAY TO DAY

You can invest a good deal of time and money to explore your behavior through all sorts of useful psychotherapy. Men, in particular have often been urged to "Get in touch with their feelings." Nothing wrong with that. It's what we do with our emotions, however, that either propels us forward or defeats us. As Tiger Woods once said, "I think the guys who are really controlling their emotions...are going to win."

So I urge you to cut through a lot of psycho clutter by understanding a very simple truth: When we live our lives according to our true and honest beliefs, we feel good. It's as simple as that. We are miserable when we choose a path that does not mirror our beliefs and values. Regret and personal disappointment occur when we make a choice that is incongruent with our personal values and beliefs.

Unhappy? You're living a life incongruent with your beliefs and values.

Happy? Your life accurately mirrors your own values and beliefs.

GOALS MUST MIRROR YOUR BELIEFS

In order to achieve a goal, your thinking, values and beliefs must be congruent with that goal. Goals and values must be consistent. They must match each other, go well together and be an expression of harmony.

INVISIBLE BREAKING BOARDS

As you know, I set the World Record by breaking through more boards in less time. No one has done this since. For me, these boards became emblematic of anything I have since had to face that might limit me. We all face personal challenges or "boards" at some point that we simply have to face and break through in order to realize our internal strength. If you have been unable to achieve certain goals, it is only because other values and beliefs—I call these invisible breaking boards—keep pushing your goals out of reach.

Most of these invisible breaking boards are like mirages. They actually don't fit reality.

They appear to be true to you. But they do not exist.

Invisible breaking boards often are embedded by misguided parents, overly critical people, and risk-adverse authority figures. We learn not to trust our abilities and original ideas. And while we often learn self-limiting beliefs from others, we also create our own invisible breaking boards, How? We exaggerate an experience. We make it worse than it is and then convince ourselves to avoid experiences that evoke the exaggerated reaction. Bitten by a bee as a child? You avoid the outdoors for the rest of your life, that sort of thing.

> Invisible breaking boards stem from erroneous thinking. They do not reflect reality.

Entire leaps of civilization and great strides by mankind have occurred because a select few chose to see real possibilities; they saw beyond mirages, misconceptions.

Perhaps a classic example of the invisible breaking board can be seen in the thousands of people who reluctantly carry on with a family business. In sum, the family business holds no interest for them. So why do they acquiesce? Because a stronger self-deceptive belief—an invisible breaking board—drives their behavior.

In this scenario, some examples of incongruent values that create invisible breaking boards might include:

My family worked hard to give me what I need; I must give back.

This job is not me. But no rush, I can always do something else later.

Any kind of work is awful, a real grind. This job is a good as any.

I hate risk. This business is a proven entity. At least it will sustain me.

That's what Thoreau meant when he wrote, "Most men lead lives of *quiet desperation* and go to the grave with the song still in them."

BREAKING BARRIERS

Two chairs on an empty porch; which chair do you choose to sit in? Like most of us, you may ease yourself into that old comfy rocker. Why not?

Yes, that comfy old rocker is a simple metaphor of what we now call a person's comfort zone. Comfort zone is a near-perfect phrase in that it sums up why all of us have a built-in resistance to change. It's uncomfortable. It's easier to rock back and forth, and watch life pass us by, right?

But sitting in a rocker does not deliver progress. It doesn't get you to where you need to be. In order to do that, you have to rise up, place one foot in front of the other and start to walk. Self-motivated people do this all the time. Others require a good deal of introspection or must have a "gut full" in order to change.

You know you want to change, right? Let's begin.

Leif Becker's Guide to Breaking Barriers

<u>Final Three Tips</u>

Own It

Whether the goal is a promotion at work, returning to college or a new exercise program, the goal must be *your* goal. Trying to fulfill another's desire lacks the self-motivation, the powerful driving force of success. Your goals must generate excitement when you visualize them. In sum, there must be something in it for you to accomplish any goal.

Realistic

Too many goals make nothing a priority. Start out with a single goal. Make it specific, attainable and reasonable. Be realistic.

Create Balance

Goals, while admirable, may focus on only one aspect of your life. If you invest an enormous amount of planning, time and energy against this one goal, there is the potential that you may throw your life out of balance. Don't succumb to tunnel vision. Instead, sustain equilibrium across all-important areas such as health, fitness, family and spirituality. New goals must drive balance in your life.

> "Without goals, and plans to reach them, you are like a ship that has set sail with no destination."
>
> —Fitzhugh Dodson

ONE FINAL NOTE

We all question the paths we've chosen and seek a better life. Several common goal-searching sessions explore questions such as:

How can I become more successful?

How can I meet my work deadlines better so I'm promoted and earn more?

How can I become happier and less anxious?

How can I lose the extra 30 pounds and fit into my good clothes?

How can I ditch this awful credit card habit and get out of debt?

Let me simplify life for you: You need not be super human to turn your goals into a reality. Most success stories require average intelligence and realistic goals.

Those who do succeed, however, embrace the following two traits.

MOTIVATION, SELF DISCIPLINE

Motivation is an individual willingness to undergo change in order to achieve a goal. Goals require change. Wanting to change is the equivalent of staying motivated. And change requires us giving up the tried and true, those things that make life comfortable.

True motivation requires leaving your comfort zone.

Self-discipline is slightly different. It equates to your willingness to work methodically and progressively toward a goal, until you achieve it. Understand that self-discipline is not complex. Think of self-discipline as a muscle; it strengthens when you use it daily. You have to practice self-discipline until it becomes second nature. Stay the course. Remain positive. Optimists view challenges and hurdles as opportunities. Self-disciplined people are optimists.

> *"We are what we repeatedly do; excellence then is not an act, but a habit."*
>
> *—Aristotle*

Expect Interruptions

John Lennon expressed it best when he said, "Life is what happens when you are busy making other plans." Expect to be faced with challenges that may try to take you off course. If you lose your step, it doesn't mean you have failed. It means you are challenged to stay the course. You and I would not be human if we were not faced with either the occasional obstacle or delightful distraction, each capable of pulling us off the path we need to be on. Expect them! Don't take them personally. Don't be caught off-guard. Work your way successfully around each challenge and remain upbeat.

Self-Disciplined Traits

Are you self-disciplined? Here is a quick glimpse into those traits that are embedded consistently in self-disciplined people:

People with discipline tend to approach tasks—even the super tough ones—with the attitude that it can be completed.

They manage finances better. They value self-reliance.

They can visualize clear results and successful conclusions.

Self-disciplined people tend not to blame others or outside circumstances for lack of success. They respect boundaries. In simplest terms, self-disciplined people do not get lots of traffic tickets, they don't get into angry snits with strangers; they do not break the rules to make life easier for them.

They have healthier relationships with loved ones.

They work through short-term highs, and can readily postpone immediate gratification. They're patient by nature.

They have a mentor or a role model whose strategies for success can be adapted. General Patton studied Hannibal to understand great war tactics. A love of learning remains a constant throughout life.

They have a strong sense of self. And feel good about who they are. They love what they do and often work and play can be interchangeable.

They have realistic goals. They don't set themselves up for failure.

When they are in a situation without joy, passion or enthusiasm, they make changes in their life rather than succumbing to negative thinking. Self-discipline gets them out of these soulless situations.

They demonstrate initiative. They understand some people are wheelbarrows who need to be filled up and pointed in the right direction. But that's not for them. They enjoy living a life that is self-directed.

Self-disciplined people can see the end result before beginning the task. They visualize. They plan. They are organized. They persevere.

NOW GET STARTED

PERFECTING THE SIMPLE ART OF SELF-DISCIPLINE

Some clients laugh when I assign this exercise. But it works. I call it "Rolling Your Way to Self-Discipline." And, if you accept that self-discipline is a muscle—it gets stronger with daily use, then you can see the simplicity—and effectiveness—of this assignment.

Use the identical approach here to any other area where self-discipline will strengthen your performance and success rate.

Look around your home and make a rough list of a dozen or so easy-to-manage chores that have been bothering you. You want to attend to them. But never do. These chores should be simple and must be able to be completed in an hour or so. Sorry, no full-day chores allowed! Examples might include:

Bringing all the loose change you've accumulated to a coin changer and simple getting the cash.

Or:

Cleaning up the tool bench in the garage; you've been busy with a lot of projects but thoughtlessly tossed the used tools back in a pile.

Do you have 12 simple tasks on your list? Here's what to do:

1. Identify your first simple chore. Make sure it can be completed in a few steps, requiring not more than an hour or so.

2. Identify a cut-off date. It can be this afternoon, tomorrow, but no more than a week away.

    Assign a meaningful penalty if you do not make this date. But give yourself a reward for getting this project done on time.

3. Make a commitment to meet the date of Project "A."

4. Before you meet that date, either today or a couple of hours before Project A's due date, identify another simple chore, Project "B" which should be a chore that may require at least as much time as the first, preferably an hour or two longer. Like weight training, you're increasing your self-discipline muscle strength.

    Assign project B's due date.

    Assign a meaningful penalty if you do not make this date. But give yourself a reward for getting this project done on time.

5. Meet Project A's date. No exceptions! Give yourself the reward and enjoy the flexing muscle of self-discipline.

6. Before Project B's due date, select another project, keeping it simple. This is Project "C." You should be able to accomplish it with about the same time investment and commitment as Project B.

Assign Project C's due date, along with the reward and penalty.

7. Meet Project B's due date and reward yourself. Before you get to Project C, identify Project D, the appropriate due date, reward and penalty and so forth.

Believe me this works!

If you put just a little muscle into it, you can be a master of your destiny. By simply addressing those small chores you chose to ignore, you "roll your way" towards perfecting the Fine Art of Self-Discipline.

"There are two things to aim at in life; first to get what you want, and after that to enjoy it. Only the wisest of mankind has achieved the second."

—Logan Pearsall Smith

WISE WORDS

Often I gain focus and direction by reading just a few short words that seem to sum up the mental boost I need. Listed below are several of my favorite quotes that have given me direction for different areas of my life. I still re-visit them from time to time.

CHARACTER

You cannot dream yourself into a character; you must hammer and forge yourself one.
Henry David Thoreau

Be your character what it will, it will be known, and nobody will take it upon your word.
Lord Chesterfield

Character is higher than intellect. A great soul will be strong to live, as well as strong to think.
Ralph Waldo Emerson

Talents are best nurtured in solitude. Character is best formed in the stormy billows of the world.
Johann Wolfgang Von Goethe

Reputation is what men and women think of us; character is what God and angels know of us.
Thomas Paine

Sow an act, and you reap a habit; sow a habit, and you reap a character; sow a character, and you reap a destiny.
George Dana Boardman

Our character is but the stamp on our souls of the free choices of good and evil we have made through life.
John C. Geikie

Character is a diamond that scratches every other stone.
Cyrus A. Bartol

Reputation is for time; character is for eternity.
J. B. Gough

A fair reputation is a plant, delicate in its nature, and by no means rapid in its growth. It will not shoot up in a night like the gourd of the prophet; but, like that gourd, it may perish in a night.
Jeremy Taylor

Let us not say, Every man is the architect of his own fortune; but let us say, Every man is the architect of his own character.
George Dana Boardman

Character is, for the most part, simply habit become fixed.
C. H. Parkhurst

The essential thing is not knowledge, but character.
Joseph Le Conte

A good name will shine forever.
Proverb

GOALS

The greatest results in life are usually attained by simple means and the exercise of ordinary qualities. These may for the most part be summed in these two: common-sense and perseverance.
Owen Feltham

The difference between a successful person and others is not a lack of strength, not a lack of knowledge, but rather a lack in will.
Vince Lombardi

Try not to become a man of success but a man of value.
Albert Einstein

If you wish success in life, make perseverance your bosom friend, experience your wise counselor, caution your elder brother, and hope your guardian genius.
Jospeph Addison

To climb steep hills requires a slow pace at first.
Shakespeare

The ability to convert ideas to things is the secret to outward success.
Henry Ward Beecher

Don't bunt. Aim out of the ballpark.
David Ogilvy

Plans miscarry because they have no aim. When a man does not know what harbor he is making for, no wind is the right wind.
Seneca

In absence of clearly defined goals, we become strangely loyal to performing daily acts of trivia.
Author Unknown

A wise man will make more opportunities than he finds.
Francis Bacon

Winning isn't everything, but wanting to win is.
Vince Lombardi

The great and glorious masterpiece of man is to know how to live to purpose.
Michel de Montaigne

The ability to concentrate and to use your time well is everything if you want to succeed in business--or almost anywhere else for that matter.
Lee Iacocca

Life can be pulled by goals just as surely as it can be pushed by drives.
Viktor Frankl

The significance of a man is not in what he attains but in what he longs to attain.
Kahlil Gibran

Every ceiling, when reached, becomes a floor, upon which one walks as a matter of course and prescriptive right.
Aldous Huxley

Ah, but a man's reach should exceed his grasp, or what's a heaven for?
Robert Browning

Nothing can stop the man with the right mental attitude from achieving his goal; nothing on earth can help the man with the wrong mental attitude.
Thomas Jefferson

SUCCESS

Success is the sum of small efforts, repeated day in and day out.
Robert Collier

Along with success comes a reputation for wisdom.
Euripides

Keep steadily before you the fact that all true success depends at last upon yourself.
Theodore T. Hunger

A failure is a man who has blundered, but is not able to cash in on the experience.
Elbert Hubbard

They can because they think they can.
Virgil

The thing always happens that you really believe in; and the belief in a thing makes it happen.
Frank Loyd Wright

FAILURE

Half of the failures in life come from pulling one's horse when he is leaping.
Thomas Hood

Our doubts are traitors, and make us lose the good we oft might win, by fearing to attempt.
William Shakespeare

It is hard to fail, but it is worse never to have tried to succeed.
Theodore Roosevelt

One who fears failure limits his activities.
Failure is only the opportunity to more intelligently begin again.
Henry Ford

Disappointments are to the soul what thunderstorms are to the air.
Johann C. F. von Schiller

Experience teaches slowly, and at the cost of mistakes.
James A. Froude

Failure is blindness to the strategic element in events; success is readiness for instant action when the opportune moment arrives.
Newell D. Hillis

What would life be if we had no courage to attempt anything?
Vincent van Gogh

Wherever we look upon this earth, the opportunities take shape within the problems.
Nelson A. Rockefeller

There is no failure except in no longer trying.
Elbert Hubbard

I was never afraid of failure, for I would sooner fail than not be among the best.
John Keats

We learn wisdom from failure much more than success. We often discover what we will do, by finding out what we will not do.
Samuel Smiles

He who fears being conquered is sure of defeat.
Napoleon Bonaparte

PERSEVERANCE

The waters wear the stones.
The Book of Job 14:19

Our greatest glory consists not in never falling, but in rising
every time we fall.
Oliver Goldsmith

Those who would attain to any marked degree of excellence
in a chosen pursuit must work, and work hard for it, prince
or peasant.
Bayard Taylor

Let me tell you the secret that has led me to my goal. My
strength lies solely in my tenacity.
Louis Pasteur

He who would do some great thing in this short life, must
apply himself to the work with such a concentration of
his forces as to the idle spectators, who live only to amuse
themselves, looks like insanity.
John Foster

Energy and persistence conquer all things.
Benjamin Franklin

It does not matter how slowly you go so long as you do not
stop.
Confucius

The block of granite which was an obstacle in the pathway of the weak, became a stepping-stone in the pathway of the strong.
Thomas Carlyle

The man who removes a mountain begins by carrying away small stones.
Chinese Proverb

The greatest mistake you can make in life is to continually be afraid you will make one.
Elbert Hubbard

GROWTH AND DEVELOPMENT

If we all did the things we are capable of,
we would astound ourselves.
Thomas Edison

Exert your talents, and distinguish yourself, and don't think
of retiring from the world, until the world will be sorry that
you retire.
Samuel Johnson

He that will not reflect is a ruined man.
Asian Proverb

Knowing yourself is the beginning of all wisdom.
Aristotle

Know thyself means this, that you get acquainted with what
you know, and what you can do.
Menander

The fact is, that to do anything in the world worth doing, we
must not stand back shivering and thinking of the cold and
danger, but jump in and scramble through as well as we can.
Robert Cushing

The only journey is the journey within.
Rainer Maria Rilke

The searching-out and thorough investigation of truth ought
to be the primary study of man.
Cicero

Make it thy business to know thyself, which is the most
difficult lesson in the world.
Miguel de Cervantes

The best rules to form a young man are: to talk little, to hear
much, to reflect alone upon what has passed in company, to
distrust one's own opinions, and value others that deserve it.
Sir William Temple

If we do not plant knowledge when young, it will give us no
shade when we are old.
Lord Chesterfield

A man who finds no satisfaction in himself will seek for it in
vain elsewhere.
La Rochefoucauld

God ever works with those who work with will.
Aeschylus

Change and growth take place when a person has risked
himself and dares to become involved with experimenting
with his own life.
Herbert Otto

Every day do something that will inch you closer to a better
tomorrow.
Doug Firebaugh

Inspiration

If you would create something,
you must be something.
Johann Wolfgang von Goethe

No great man ever complains of want of opportunities.
Ralph Waldo Emerson

Do we not all agree to call rapid thought and noble impulse
by the name of inspiration?
George Eliot

First say to yourself what you would be;
and then do what you have to do.
Epictetus

Men do less than they ought,
unless they do all they can.
Thomas Carlyle

If you can imagine it, you can achieve it; if you can dream it,
you can become it.
William Arthur Ward

DREAMS

*Happy are those who dream dreams and are ready to pay
the price to make them come true.*
Leon J. Suenes

*The end of wisdom is to dream high enough not to lose the
dream in the seeking of it.*
William Faulkner

*Go confidently in the direction of your dreams. Live the life
you have imagined.*
Henry David Thoreau

Hope is the dream of the waking man.
French Proverb

*All men dream but not equally. Those who dream by night
in the dusty recesses of their minds wake in the day to find
that it was vanity; but the dreamers of the day are dangerous
men, for they may act their dream with open eyes to make it
possible.*
T.E. Lawrence

*The question for each man to settle is not what he would do
if he had means, time, influence and educational advantages;
the question is what he will do with the things he has. The
moment a young man ceases to dream or to bemoan his lack
of opportunities and resolutely looks his conditions in the
face, and resolves to change them, he lays the corner-stone of
a solid and honorable success.*
Hamilton Wright Mabie

Commitment leads to action. Action brings your dream closer.
Marcia Wieder

The best way to make your dreams come true is to wake up.
Paul Valery

The future belongs to those who believe in the beauty of their dreams.
Eleanor Roosevelt

The following are quotes from Bruce Lee. Known for his martial arts, Bruce Lee was also a great philosopher –

Bruce Lee Quotes

Real living is living for others.

If you love life, don't waste time, for time is what life is made up of.

I am not teaching you anything. I just help you to explore yourself.

If you always put a limit on everything you do, physical or anything else. It will spread into your work and into your life. There are no limits. There are only plateaus, and you must not stay there, you must go beyond them.

I fear not the man who has practiced 10,000 kicks once, but I fear the man who has practiced one kick 10,000 times.

Ever since I was a child I have had this instinctive urge for expansion and growth. To me, the function and duty of a quality human being is the sincere and honest development of one's potential.

As long as I can remember I feel I have had this great creative and spiritual force within me that is greater than faith, greater than ambition, greater than confidence, greater than determination, greater than vision. It is all these combined. My brain becomes magnetized with this dominating force which I hold in my hand.

The possession of anything begins in the mind.

It's not the daily increase but daily decrease. Hack away at the unessential.

Love is like a friendship caught on fire. In the beginning a flame, very pretty, often hot and fierce, but still only light and flickering. As love grows older, our hearts mature and our love becomes as coals, deep-burning and unquenchable.

NOTES

NOTES

NOTES

NOTES

NOTES

NOTES

NOTES

NOTES

NOTES

NOTES

For more information on Leif
Becker's seminars, workshops
and products please visit:
www.LeifBecker.com